TEACHER TRAINING AND PROFESSIONAL DEVELOPMENT OF CHINESE ENGLISH LANGUAGE TEACHERS

This up-close look at Chinese ESL teachers documents undertakings at formal and informal levels to support and sustain their expertise in ways that balance collaborative and competitive efforts, situated and standards-based programs, ethnically responsive and government-based efforts, and traditional and 21st-century teaching visions. English is a mandated subject for approximately 400 million Chinese public school students. Making transparent the training and professional development received respectively by pre-service and in-service teachers, this book provides a rare window into how Chinese English Language teachers (ELTs) reconcile the two needs with the responsibility to teach large numbers of students while also navigating societal, cultural, and institutional cross currents. It also explores the range of ways China invests in the training and professional development of its English language teachers.

Faridah Pawan is a professor in ESL/EFL teacher education in the Department of Literacy, Culture, and Language Education in the School of Education at Indiana University, USA.

Wenfang Fan is a professor in the Department of Foreign Languages at Tsinghua University, People's Republic of China.

Miao Pei is an associate professor in language pedagogy at the Center for Teacher Education Research in the Faculty of Education at Beijing Normal University, People's Republic of China.

ESL & Applied Linguistics Professional Series
Eli Hinkel, Series Editor

Reflective Practice in English Language Teaching
Research-Based Principles and Practices
Mann/Walsh

Teacher Training and Professional Development of Chinese English Language Teachers
Changing From Fish to Dragon
Pawan/Fan/Pei, Eds.

Corrective Feedback in Second Language Teaching and Learning
Research, Theory, Applications, Implications
Nassaji/Kartchava, Eds.

Teaching Writing for Academic Purposes to Multilingual Students
Instructional Approaches
Bitchener/Storch/Wette, Eds.

Family Language Policies in a Multilingual World
Opportunities, Challenges, and Consequences
Macalister/Mirvahedi, Eds.

Handbook of Research in Second Language Teaching and Learning, Volume III
Hinkel, Ed.

Visit **www.routledge.com/education** for additional information on titles in the ESL & Applied Linguistics Professional Series

TEACHER TRAINING AND PROFESSIONAL DEVELOPMENT OF CHINESE ENGLISH LANGUAGE TEACHERS

Changing From Fish to Dragon

Faridah Pawan, Wenfang Fan, and Miao Pei

With Ge Wang, Wei Jin, Xin Chen, and Niya Yuan

NEW YORK AND LONDON

First published 2017
by Routledge
711 Third Avenue, New York, NY 10017

and by Routledge
2 Park Square, Milton Park, Abingdon, Oxon, OX14 4RN

Routledge is an imprint of the Taylor & Francis Group, an informa business

© 2017 Taylor & Francis

The right of Faridah Pawan, Wenfang Fan, and Miao Pei to be identified as the authors of the editorial material, and of the authors for their individual chapters, has been asserted in accordance with sections 77 and 78 of the Copyright, Designs and Patents Act 1988.

All rights reserved. No part of this book may be reprinted or reproduced or utilized in any form or by any electronic, mechanical, or other means, now known or hereafter invented, including photocopying and recording, or in any information storage or retrieval system, without permission in writing from the publishers.

Trademark notice: Product or corporate names may be trademarks or registered trademarks, and are used only for identification and explanation without intent to infringe.

Library of Congress Cataloging-in-Publication Data
A catalog record for this book has been requested

ISBN: 978-1-138-12449-3 (hbk)
ISBN: 978-1-138-12451-6 (pbk)
ISBN: 978-1-315-64811-8 (ebk)

Typeset in Bembo
by Apex CoVantage, LLC

CONTENTS

List of Contributors   vii
Acknowledgments   ix

Introduction: Situating Chinese English Language Teacher Training and Professional Development in Research and Policy   1
Faridah Pawan

1 "Filling the Pail Before the Cup": Preparing to Be a Teacher   10
Miao Pei, Faridah Pawan, and Wei Jin

2 Student Teaching: "All the Sour, Sweet, Bitter, and Pungent Flavors Must Be Tested"   28
Miao Pei and Wei Jin

3 Permanent Teacher Qualifications: "Surviving Within the Iron Rice Bowl"   41
Wenfang Fan, Ge Wang, and Xin Chen

4 Master-Novice (Shifu-Tudi) Teacher Relationships: Acquiring Knowledge From the Backbone of Experience   51
Wenfang Fan

5 School-Based Professional Development With
  "Jiaoyanzu" Peers: Learning With Brothers and Sisters 64
  Faridah Pawan and Wenfang Fan

6 High-Stakes Public Teaching Competitions: Failure Is Not
  Falling but Failure Is Not Getting up From Each Fall 81
  Faridah Pawan

7 The National Guo Pei Project for Rural Teachers:
  Opening Doors So That Others May Enter 97
  Miao Pei and Wei Jin

8 English Teacher Development in Rural and Ethnically
  Diverse Areas: Sowers Action Seeding the Fields 111
  Ge Wang

9 The Visiting Scholars Program: Adding a Flower to
  a Brocade 125
  Faridah Pawan and Xin Chen

10 New Chinese Education Reform Targets English:
   U.S. and Chinese Scholars' Perspectives 141
   Faridah Pawan and Niya Yuan

Index *149*

CONTRIBUTORS

Faridah Pawan is Professor of ESL/EFL Teacher Education in the Department of Literacy, Culture & Language Education (LCLE) in the School of Education, Indiana University. Her current research are in the informal and formal approaches of ESL/EFL teacher education and professional development; ESL and Content Area Teacher collaborative professional development; and hybrid and online teaching pedagogy. Her funded research projects are located in school districts in Indiana in the U.S, in Beijing and Kunming in China, and in Istanbul, Turkey. She has published widely in journals such as TESOL Quarterly, Teaching and Teacher Education, Language Learning and Technology and Journal of Ethnographic and Qualitative Research. This book is her fourth book on language teacher education and professional development (www.fpawan.com)

Wenfang Fan is Professor of Linguistics and Applied Linguistics in the Department of Languages and Literatures, Tsinghua University. Her research is in Applied Linguistics with a specific focus on ESL/EFL instruction of Chinese students and in functional linguistics. As one of the leading figures in English Language Teacher (ELT) reform in China, she has been undertaking a research project called, The Dragon of ELT Reform Project, involving experimental schools nationwide in China. Her English textbooks for public schools are authorized by the Chinese National Department of Education and used in public schools all over China. She has also published articles in the fields of ESL/EFL and functional linguistics.

Pei Miao is Associate Professor of teacher education and language pedagogy in Center for Teacher Education Research in Faculty of Education, Beijing Normal University, Beijing, People's Republic of China. Her current research are in teacher learning and development, second language learning and teaching. Her research projects are located in schools in Beijing, Chongqing, Yunnan province and similar rural and ethnic minority areas in China. She has published widely in Chinese journals such as Teacher Education Research, Comparative Education Review, Educational Research and Experiment; and international journals such as The Modern Language Journal, Foreign Language Annals, Asia Pacific Educational Review. This book on teacher education and professional development, is her second but her first book in English.

Ge Wang is Professor of Applied Linguistics at School of Foreign Languages, Zhongnan University of Economics and Law, China. He has been engaged in English teaching and research in multilingual education in Yunnan over 20 years. He obtained his PhD in English Language Education from the University of Hong Kong and was the 2014-2015 Sino-American Fulbright research visiting scholar at Graduate School of Education, the University of Pennsylvania. His research interest is in applied linguistics, bi/trilingual education, intercultural communication and educational anthropology. His major publications can be found in the internationally refereed journals such as The Journal of Asia TEFL, International Journal of Bilingual Education and Bilingualism (SSCI), The Asia-Pacific Education Researcher (SSCI) and book chapters published by TESOL, Routledge, Springer and John Benjamins. He is currently the deputy secretary of Yunnan Foreign Language Education Association (YFLEA) and Vice director of International Association of Multilingual Education, Yunnan Branch (IAME Yunnan Branch).

Xin Chen is a doctoral student at Indiana University. She received her B.A in English Language and Literature from Fudan University, China and obtained her MSc in Management from University of Edinburgh, UK. Now Xin is pursuing a Ph.D. in Literacy, Culture and Language Education with a minor in Management and Entrepreneurship. She is also an associate instructor of first-year composition to multilingual students at Indiana University. Her research area is English academic literacy education for multilingual students and international education. She has presented her research in conferences in the field such as the National Council of Teachers of English Assembly for Research and TESOL.

Wei Jin is a doctoral student at Center for Teacher Education Research, Faculty of Education, Beijing Normal University, Beijing, People's Republic of China. His major research interests are teacher self-studies of teaching and teacher education practice, and pedagogy of teacher education. He had been an English Teacher for almost 8 years in a variety of schools and institutions before going into his current field of research.

Niya Yuan is a lecturer in the School of Foreign Languages at Harbin University of Science and Technology, People's Republic of China. She is completing a doctorate with Beijing Normal University. She was a visiting scholar in the 2014-2015 academic year, at the School of Education, Indiana University, Bloomington, Indiana, U.S.A. Her research interests are EFL pedagogy, EFL teacher knowledge and professional development.

ACKNOWLEDGMENTS

We thank our English language teacher colleagues most sincerely. They move mountains and make a difference daily through their hard work and dedication to their students and to their profession.

We thank Naomi Silverman at Routledge/Taylor & Francis and Eli Hinkel, Series Editor for the ESL & Applied Linguistics Professional Series, for their steadfast belief in and empathetic support of our writing endeavors. All authors should have the privilege of working with these two vibrant women.

We also thank our family members who tolerate us spending many late nights working and many days away from home pursuing our research.

We also thank each other for the collaboration to make this book possible. As the Chinese saying goes, when everyone puts their share of firewood into the fire, flames from it rise high and bright.

Faridah Pawan, Wenfang Fan, Miao Pei,
Ge Wang, Wei Jin, Xin Chen, and Niya Yuan

INTRODUCTION

Situating Chinese English Language Teacher Training and Professional Development in Research and Policy

Faridah Pawan

The Chinese saying, "Changing from fish to dragon" (鲤鱼跳龙门, Li Yu Tiao Long Men) has cultural/mythological roots representing courage, perseverance, and accomplishment. The saying is based on an old and enduring image of a carp fish jumping over a gate put up by a dragon, a mythical creature symbolizing a great Chinese Emperor. The "Dragon's Gate" is located at the top of a waterfall which is cascading down from a legendary mountain. Many carp fish swim upstream against the strong currents of the waterfall, but few are strong, brave, and persistent enough to make the final leap over the waterfall. When a carp fish is finally successful in making the difficult jump, it is transformed into a powerful dragon.

The five-character expression of the saying was once used to show pride and respect for a person's success in passing very difficult examinations, required of citizens who aspire to enter into the imperial administrative service. To this day, the expression is used to describe achievements over difficult circumstances and to express the ideal that if a person works hard and diligently, success will one day be achieved.

In the spirit of the story, this book captures the diligent work of Chinese English teachers (ELTs) to attain and maintain their expertise and professional stature. Its main purpose is to provide insight into how the ELTs develop and maintain their teaching skills, a process that is challenging and requires extensive efforts on the part of the teachers. Although there are about 1,126,696 (Decision of the CCCP, 2014) Chinese ELTs, approximately 400 million Chinese public school students are studying English. The faculty to student ratio comes to about 1 ELT for each 400 students.

At the global level, the discussion of Chinese ELTs is important as they fall within the non-native English speaker teacher (NNEST) workforce who comprise

80% of the individuals who teach English in the profession (Braine, 2013). NNESTs have different needs as well as abilities than native speaking English teachers. Understanding what these needs are for Chinese ELTs will contribute to a broader understanding of how to support the professional development of this large segment of the ELT workforce.

The research reported here is a collaboration between U.S. and Chinese colleagues (Faridah Pawan, Wenfang Fan, Miao Pei, and Ge Wang) who are all language teacher educators at their respective institutions. Our graduate students, Xin Chen and Wei Jin, are also critical members of the collaborative team as is Niya Yuan, Pawan's visiting scholar. We undertook the research through our participation in fifteen professional development sessions that we organized or were invited to participate in, at urban and rural school districts concentrated primarily in the Northwestern provinces but also in selected schools in the Northeast, Southeast, and Southwest of China. As we participated in the sessions, we conducted needs analyses, individual and focus group interviews (both online and onsite), observed classroom teaching and analyzed documents (e.g., syllabi, lesson plans, school policies and government policies, annual reports) that impact teachers in the districts. From the interviews, we were able to obtain information on teachers' training needs as well as the types of professional development they seek and are available to them. Classroom observations consolidated information on areas to be addressed. Document analyses yielded information on official requirements and the types of support available to teachers within their schools and beyond. These methods provided a means to triangulate and validate information.

From these undertakings, we were also able to gain insight into and critique teacher training in "normal"/teaching university preparation programs for pre-service teachers (Chapters 1 and 2); teacher permanent employment qualifications (Chapter 3), experienced- and novice-teacher relationships (Chapter 4), professional development for in-service teachers that are peer- and competition-based (Chapters 5 and 6), professional development efforts in the rural and ethnically diverse areas (Chapters 7 and 8) as well as professional development overseas in the Chinese Visiting Scholars Program (Chapter 9). In Chapter 10, we end the book by discussing the future of teacher training and professional development for Chinese ELTs, in light of a new national reform initiative that targets the English language.

Critical Juncture

The focus on teacher training and professional development efforts in this book comes at a critical juncture for teachers of all subject areas, including those teaching English as a second/foreign language (ESL/EFL). During times of professional vulnerability, especially those brought about by political and economic uncertainties, their professionalism is constantly challenged. Thus, a discussion of the complex issues surrounding the situation is necessary as it can provide backdrop to the opportunities and challenges that exist for the training and professional development of teachers in general and for Chinese ELTs in particular in this book.

First and foremost, how does the public perceive teaching and teacher expertise at this point in time? Is teaching as a profession devoid of "specialized, systematic, rigorous and scientific" (Tsui, 2003, p. 16) knowledge because it is such a common practice and a common experience for anyone who has been in school? Is it a "lower-status" profession because it is only a matter of conveying or applying information from elsewhere? Those who hold these views lack awareness of research on the role that teachers play in actively constructing knowledge, along with their students, as they encounter, reflect, and explore new information and new dimensions of understanding (see Schön, 1983; Shulman, 1987; Cochran-Smith & Lytle, 1993; Clandinin, Connelly & Craig, 1995; Verloop, Van Driel & Meijer, 2001; Johnson, 2006; Korthagen, 2010).

Teacher knowledge is dialectical knowledge in that it develops, evolves, and is mediated by what teachers know about the subject matter, about themselves as people and as learners, about their students, about the learning that is taking place in their classroom, about the micro school culture in which they work and the community in which they and their students live (see Johnson, 2006). Grangeat (2008, p. 2) notes the importance of understanding the uniqueness and situatedness of teacher knowledge; it is a complex "synthesis between knowledge which results from education and that which follows lived experiences." Specifically, teacher professional knowledge is derived from the work process itself; it results from the exchanges amongst all stakeholders committed to the profession and the institutions and the communities they are a part of. Thus, in this perspective, knowledge is understood to be a component and product of the collective culture where the teaching is undertaken.

These factors require teachers and teacher trainers to "reconceptualize and recontextualize their understanding" (Johnson & Golombek, 2003, p. 735) of all aspects of teaching and learning. Possessing subject matter knowledge (theoretical/applied linguistics and English language knowledge, in the case of language teachers) is, of course, essential. But equally important for achieving effective teaching and learning is understanding how knowledge is communicated and understood by teachers and students and how context influences the transmission and interpretation of knowledge in the classroom.

In this regard, "praxis" is a defining element in teacher expertise in that subject matter knowledge, practice, and context dialectically inform one other in the minds and actions of teachers. It also involves what Freeman (2009) would add as teachers' continued growth as "socio-professionals." Teachers substantiate and expand their praxis to include interactions with stakeholders beyond their own immediate school environs. The relationship between subject matter knowledge, practical experience, and societal engagement create a "teacher knowledge construct" or belief system that distinguishes teachers in meaningful ways from other professionals.

This book also comes at a time when teacher de-professionalization dominates public and political discourse on education in general. One source for the conundrum is the frequent confusion between professionalization and professionalism. Focusing on ESL/EFL teachers, Crandall (1993) asserts that professionalization is a time-limited "status enhancement through certification or credentialing, contracts, and tenure" (pp. 499–500) while professionalism is a life-long learning process that teachers undertake to enhance the quality of their professional practice. When professionalization is seen as the goal of training and professional development, the focus of the effort is to standardize credentials by ordaining the quantity and type of knowledge pre- and in-service teachers should have. What this approach ignores are the elements that contribute to teacher "professionalism," i.e., teachers' quest to experience and be exposed to intellectual work that accompanies their practice; to refine their judgment and sense of ethics through extended specialized training; and to assume autonomy and assert their rights as professionals to control their own practice (see Raelin, 1989; Yeom & Ginsburg, 2007). As Darling-Hammond (1985, p. 205) stresses, teacher "professionalism goes beyond the issues of status and compensation of the members of an occupation; it implies the members of an occupational group strive for informed perspective and practice, for both public recognition and respect through accountability that the latter holds in high regard, and for full control over their work."

The current discourse that challenges teachers as professionals can be understood through the concept of "threat rigidity" (Olsen & Sexton, 2009) stemming from "an organization, when perceiving itself under siege (i.e. threatened or in crisis), responds in identifiable ways: structures are tightened; centralized control increases; conformity is stressed; accountability and efficiency measures are emphasized; and alternative and innovative thinking is discouraged" (p. 15). Threat rigidity is a concept that has a place in the current highly competitive and politicized global economy in China and the U.S. where teacher education in both countries is entrenched in the discussions of the countries' national and global aspirations.

Within the context of these perspectives, policies impacting teachers in both countries need to be explored. They can provide a good indicator as to whether or not teachers are being used as easy scapegoats for the threats, fears, and misconceptions that prevail during the current times of change and uncertainty.

Chinese and U.S. Teacher Policies in Perspective

Chinese and U.S. governmental policies and actions set the tone for how teachers are perceived and how their professionalism is understood in this current environment. The priorities placed on China's national economic development present both huge opportunities and challenges for educational reform and changes. Since Deng Xiaoping announced the Four Modernization and Open-Door Policy in 1978, China's economic growth rate accelerated rapidly to 15 percent annually at its highest in the mid-eighties. A new and more modest goal of 6.5 percent annual growth by 2020 nevertheless underlines the nation's confidence in its continued growth. In this context "teachers are regarded as the key factor in the reforms . . . and amongst all the stakeholders . . . the Chinese government has the most direct and frequent influences on teachers work by enacting policies" (Wang, 2012, p. 17) that directly affect them. Wang's (2012) analysis of three central government documents is illustrative. The 1993 Teacher Law is the first formal document that states that teachers are specialists with a specific expertise to offer. In 1995, the Teacher Certification Regulations contain requirements such as Chinese citizenship, and credentials such as academic diplomas, documented support from officials, and success in examinations, in order to be able to assume any teaching position. In 1999, the Regulations of Teacher Continued Education Act delineate that teacher professional development must consist of content determined by policy makers and that is aligned with ongoing educational reforms. These documents and policies drive teacher preparation and professional development at all levels of education in China.

The directives that have emerged from these governmental mandates take place in the context of frequently changing policies and requirements for English language instruction as a subject. In 1978, after the Cultural Revolution temporarily suspended its practice, English language teaching resumed and the language was re-instated as a compulsory subject in Chinese public schools. At the tertiary level a 1993 pilot reform plan called "3 + 2" promoted English as one of the five core college-entrance examination subjects. Subsequently, the status of English in China also benefitted from heightened expectations for international engagement (Hu, 2005). These have been fueled by the country's 1998 acceptance into the World Trade Organization (WTO), its success in hosting the 2008 Olympic Games, its status since 2010 as the world's second-largest economy, and in 2015, the inclusion of the Chinese yuan as one of the five world's reserve currencies in the International Monetary Fund (IMF). Nevertheless, as of late 2015, China's national policy toward English appears to have shifted (see Chapter 10). Similar to other shifts in English language policies, the policy in 2015 has created uncertainty among Chinese ELTs about how the profession will be valued in China in the future.

These new policies translate into a form of "demanded professionalism" (Wang, 2012, p. 18) in which the central government, and not the teachers themselves, has the most influence and power over shaping the profession; teacher professionalism in the sense described previously is diminished. Wang (2012) argues that the government's policy has focused on teachers' ability to perform in a narrow and specific area of economic competitiveness. The focus is evident as a means to ensure that the country is able to not only compete but also to have an edge over other countries. Such an environment places teachers in the position of deliverers and enforcers of governmental values and goals.

U.S. governmental teacher policies incrementally diminish teachers' professionalism over the years and have the effect of driving them away from the profession because they reduce the teachers to over-regulated cogs in the larger political machinery. The impetus for the teacher policies can be traced to U.S. students' underperformance in international standardized tests such as the Third International Mathematics and Science Study (TIMSS) and Program for International Student Assessment (PISA) in which U.S. students have seldom shown excellent performance in relation to their counterparts in other countries. Instead of problematizing the nature of the tests themselves and acknowledging what U.S. students have been able to achieve despite the tests, teachers have been blamed for what is perceived as their inability to train and prepare students, specifically in mathematics and science, in order to be globally competitive (Kumashiro, 2012). This is evident in the 1983 "A Nation at Risk" report by the National Commission on Excellence in Education:

> Our nation is at risk. Our once unchallenged pre-eminence in commerce, industry, science, and technological innovation is being overtaken by competitors throughout the world. . . . others are matching and surpassing our educational attainments.
>
> *(p. 5)*

The committee had twelve members, with only one teacher on the commission and no other educational experts on board. Not surprisingly, it has triggered many of the policies that teachers have struggled with ever since. In these policies, primacy is placed on (1) high-stakes testing, (2) scripted curricula, and (3) fast-track teacher training (Milner, 2013). In 2001, President G. W. Bush's No Child Left Behind (NCLB) policy specified that teacher accountability and performance are tied to all learners achieving the pre-defined and limited goal of high scores in high-stakes tests within a specified time, regardless of the students' differences in backgrounds and starting points. The intense and overarching focus on this goal (non-achievement could lead to teacher job loss) generally forced teachers to follow narrowed and scripted curricula as roadmaps to test success. Unfortunately, scripted curricula had also inadvertently come to define President Obama's 2009 implementation of the Race to the Top (RTTP) grant programs through their focus on alternative and fast-tracked teacher training. The rush to qualify teachers in areas of need had given preference to programs such as Teach for America (TFA) where pedagogical training is limited and can be as minimal as a few weeks of training. It is not surprising then that criticisms of the programs include complaints of teacher recruits' over-reliance on prescribed instructions to the detriment of instruction tailored to the needs of individual students (both high-achieving and low-achieving). The situation is compounded by executive support of the Common Core Standards initially developed during President Reagan's administration (1981–1989) requiring teachers to abide by externally prescribed content and standards in instruction. The Every Student Succeeds Act (ESSA) signed on December 10, 2015, will take effect in the 2017–2018 school year. The policy is aimed at giving states more control and influence in setting educational policies. Of most relevance to the discussion in this book is one of the Act's policies involving the U.S. federal government's relegation of the responsibility for evaluating teachers to the states themselves. It remains to be seen as to how teachers will be impacted and whether the Act will provide the much needed boost to teachers' efforts to acquire and sustain their professionalism. At this point in time, there is also a great deal of insecurity about ESSA's implementation under the Trump administration, with Betsy DeVos as the newly appointment Education Secretary.

In the meantime, uncertainty about the teaching profession and disdain by teachers on its over-regulation have led many prospective and active teachers to shy away from it. Teacher training programs around the country are reporting anywhere from a 20–50% drop in enrollment of prospective teachers as students (Westervelt, 2015) and a severe shortage of teachers is in the pipeline.

It is clear that in the U.S., as in China, teachers' professionalism is influenced and takes place within a social and political context. Teacher professionalism is thus not an absolute but rather is a "socially constructed, contextually variable and contested concept" (Troman cited in Wang, 2012, p. 18).

The Purpose of This Book: A Focus on Chinese ELTs

The authors in this book describe several national and local level professional development initiatives in China. In doing so, the book provides insight into the environment in which they take place and how these undertakings impact English language teachers' (ELTs) sense of professionalism. In perusing the chapters, it may be of use to readers to keep in mind elements that Hodkinson and Hodkinson (2005, p. 124) identify as those supportive of teachers, their growth in training and professional development programs, namely:

- Close collaborative working environments;
- Colleagues [being] mutually supportive in enhancing teacher learning;
- Supported opportunities for personal development that go beyond school or government priorities;
- Out-of-school educational opportunities including time to stand back, reflect and think differently;
- Opportunities to integrate off-the-job learning into everyday practice;
- Opportunities to extend professional identity through boundary crossing into other departments, school activities, schools and beyond.

Several of these elements will be emerge as strong and defining elements in the Chinese ELTs' contexts while others are either in progress or do not yet exist.

References

Braine, G. (2013). *Non-native educators in English language teaching.* New York: Routledge.
Clandinin, D. J., Connelly, F. M., & Craig, C. (1995). *Teachers' professional knowledge landscapes.* New York: Teachers College Press.
Cochran-Smith, M., & Lytle, S. L. (Eds.). (1993). *Inside/outside: Teacher research and knowledge.* New York: Teachers College Press.
Crandall, J. (1993). Professionalism and professionalization of adult ESL literacy. *TESOL Quarterly, 27*(3), 497–515.
Darling-Hammond, L. (1985). Valuing teachers: The making of a profession. *Teachers College Record, 87*(2), 205.
Decision of the CCCP on some major issues concerning comprehensively deepening the reform. (2014). Retrieved from www.china.org.cn/chinese/2014-01/17/content_31226494_12.htm
Freeman, D. (2009). The scope of second language teacher education. In A. Burns & J. C. Richards (Eds.), *The Cambridge guide to second language teacher education* (pp. 11–19). Cambridge, UK: Cambridge University Press.
Grangeat, M. (2008). *Complexity of teachers' knowledge: A synthesis between personal goals, collective culture and conceptual knowledge.* Paper presented at Network 10—Teacher Education Research, European Conference on Educational Research (ECER), Gothenburg, Sweden. Retrieved from www.leeds.ac.uk/educol/documents/176227.pdf
Hodkinson, H., & Hodkinson, P. (2005). Improving school teachers' workplace learning. *Research Papers in Education, 20*(2), 109–131.
Hu, G. (2005). English language education in China: Policies, progress, and problems. *Language Policy, 4*(1), 5–24.
Johnson, K. E. (2006). The sociocultural turn and its challenges for second language teacher education. *TESOL Quarterly, 40*(1), 235–257.
Johnson, K. E., & Golombek, P. R. (2003). "Seeing" teacher learning. *TESOL Quarterly, 37*(4), 729–737.
Korthagen, F. A. (2010). Situated learning theory and the pedagogy of teacher education: Towards an integrative view of teacher behavior and teacher learning. *Teaching and Teacher Education, 26*(1), 98–106.
Kumashiro, K. (2012). *Bad teacher! How blaming teachers distorts the bigger picture.* New York: Teachers College Press.
Milner, H. R. (2013). *Policy reforms and de-professionalization of teaching.* Boulder, CO: National Education Policy Center.
National Commission on Excellence in Education. (1983). *A nation at risk: A report to the nation and the secretary of education.* Washington, DC: US Department of Education.
Olsen, B., & Sexton, D. (2009). Threat rigidity, school reform, and how teachers view their work inside current education policy contexts. *American Educational Research Journal, 46*(1), 9–44. doi: 10.3102/0002831208320573
Raelin, J. A. (1989). Unionization and deprofessionalization: Which comes first? *Journal of Organizational Behavior, 10*(2), 101–115.
Schön, D. A. (1983). *The reflective practitioner: How professionals think in action.* New York: Basic Books.
Shulman, L. (1987). Knowledge and teaching: Foundations of the new reform. *Harvard Educational Review, 57*(1), 1–23.
Tsui, A. B. M. (2003). *Understanding expertise in teaching.* New York: Cambridge University Press.

Verloop, N., Van Driel, J., & Meijer, P. (2001). Teacher knowledge and the knowledge base of teaching. *International Journal of Educational Research, 35*(5), 441–461.

Wang, X. (2012). Demanded professionalism: Discourse analysis of state policy on teacher professionalism in Mainland China. *Journal of Cambridge Studies, 7*(2), 17. Retrieved from http://dx.doi.org/10.17863/CAM.1422

Westervelt, E. (2015, August 15). Teacher shortage? Or teacher pipeline problem? *nprEd*. Retrieved from www.npr.org/sections/ed/2015/08/19/432724094/teacher-shortage-or-teacher-pipeline-problem

Yeom, M., & Ginsburg, M. (2007). Professionalism and the reform of teachers and teacher education in the Republic of Korea & the United States of America. *Asia Pacific Education Review, 8*(2), 298–310. doi: 10.1007/bf03029264

1
"FILLING THE PAIL BEFORE THE CUP"

Preparing to Be a Teacher

Miao Pei, Faridah Pawan, and Wei Jin

Introduction

The traditional philosophies of Daoism and Confucianism have permeated Chinese ideas about education. These philosophies provide a foundation for understanding interconnections between the pursuit of knowledge and teaching which the Chinese view as virtuous callings.

Dao means "The Way" toward high rewards and a sense of fulfillment through the search for truth. The quest for truth in Daoism should be undertaken with naturalness, spontaneity, and simplicity. Adherents strive to be in harmony with nature and one another. Laozi, the founder of this school of thought, often used "water" as a metaphor to describe this pursuit in that it nurtures and brings good to all. Like water, what is gained becomes a part of us all as human beings, never to be altered or changed but allowed to course naturally through life. In its most basic meaning, Daoism is considered to be the understanding of truth that humans gain in the pursuit of "The Way." Teaching is considered the primary means of achieving this goal as well as a means to enable others to engage in the pursuit. It is considered not an objective skill or technique but rather an art. This is because like water, there are indeterminate ways for teachers to reach and connect with students through their teaching. It takes knowledge and experience to do it just right.

Confucianism has also greatly influenced teaching and learning in China. In particular, Confucianism puts the teacher and teaching as the most noble of responsibilities. Confucius is most known for his virtuous humility, because he credits his ancestors with all that he knows and understands. Thus, it is not surprising that he placed at the very top, amongst the five most ideal of relationships, the relationship between a father and his reverent son in addition to ruler-citizen, husband-wife, older-younger brother, and friend-friend. In the father-son relationship, the son learns from the father by being obedient, loyal, and accepting of his father's words, instructions, and knowledge.

Confucius is also known for his pragmatic and structured advice. In his view, individuals can only be teachers after they possess knowledge. Before they practice their craft, teachers must be learners first who must memorize and become familiar with the words and wisdom of those who came before them. Upon doing so, they must revise and make modifications to it using experiences and knowledge that have been gained through work and study. All these activities should bring satisfaction, fulfillment, and pleasure in being a learned teacher (学而时习之，不亦说乎). These philosophies are in evidence in today's teacher education models in China where subject matter acquisition receives top priority and where teaching practice is considered an application of knowledge obtained from training. Finally, practice and experience as to what is possible and achievable in the classroom completes the professional development of teachers.

Daoism and Confucianism provide a background to the philosophical mindset behind the preparation of pre-service Chinese English language teachers discussed in this chapter. We begin first by looking at the various institutions that prepare teachers in training. We then discuss the most recent English language standards for Chinese students published in 2011 since these serve as the basis of pre-service teachers' training. We will then explore the teacher training curricula offered at training institutions which reveal what teacher educators' strategies are for achieving the goals of the 2011 standards. Finally, we report on interviews with former and current pre-service teachers regarding their teacher preparation experiences in relation to the standards and the curricula included in this chapter.

The Pathways to Pre-Service Teacher Preparation

In China, the teaching mission is undertaken by three types of institutions, namely through normal schools, teacher colleges, and normal universities (Zhu, 2015). Normal schools are for candidates interested in becoming kindergarten teachers. These schools are usually managed and run by the local government at the city level. Examples of these schools include Shandong Wendeng Normal School, Nanyang Normal School, and Beijing Tongxian Normal School. Middle school teachers are graduates of teacher colleges such as Nanyang Teachers College, Anyang Teachers College, and Luoyang Teachers College. (Although these are teaching colleges, they can at times identify themselves as provincial universities as well.) Individuals who want to teach at the high school level have to attend normal universities or comprehensive universities in the departments of education. Four of the most highly ranked universities for this purpose are Beijing Normal University, East China Normal University, Northeast Normal University, and Central China Normal University (see Table 1.1).

TABLE 1.1 Teacher Training Institutions

	No. of teacher candidates	Applicants' qualifications	Location	Number of years in each institution	Degrees	Teaching levels
Normal schools	38,709	Junior Middle School graduates with zhongkao scores	In small cities, and even in the country	3 years	专科 (zhuanke)	Kindergarten
Teacher colleges	203,330	Junior Middle School graduates with zhongkao scores or High School with gaokao scores	In medium-sized cities	4 or 3 + 2 years or other configurations based on provincial systems	专科 (zhuanke) or bachelor degree	Junior Middle School or High School
Normal universities	177,778	High School graduates with gaokao scores	In medium- to large-sized cities	4 or 4 + 2 years, depending on the type of degree sought	bachelor degree/ master's degree or a doctorate	High School/ College or University

Source: Center for Teacher Education Research. (2016). *A survey report of Chinese Teacher Education.*

This classification of teacher training institutions is at the most general level. The situation on the ground is more complex; further classifications can be made as to where students can seek their educational preparation for teaching. In fact, teacher education is open to all institutions willing to undertake it. Thus, in addition to "normal" institutions whose expressed missions are to prepare teachers, teacher education departments can also be found in comprehensive four-year universities, comprehensive colleges, vocational colleges, and "dependent" institutes affiliated with key universities (e.g., Minsheng College affiliated with Henan University).

In 2007, the State Council, a body governing all issues including education for each province in China, directed five key normal universities (Beijing Normal University, Northeast Normal University, East China Normal University, Shaanxi Normal University, and Southwest University) to admit students from rural areas free of charge. The condition is that the students are to return to teach in their hometowns for at least ten years. The government's aim, as expressed by Wen Jiabao, China's ex-premier, is to develop and promote educational equity by increasing access to education for teachers from these areas through this tuition waiver (Yao & Chen, 2009, p. 63). (See also Pei & Jin's Chapter 7 and Wang's Chapter 8.)

English Language Standards as Targets for Teacher Preparation

The Chinese Ministry of Education (MOE) introduced English Language Curriculum Standards in 2003 in an experimental form before releasing the new edited version in 2011 (MOE, 2011). There are nine levels of English language competency objectives and teachers use them as guides in their curricular design. English instruction begins at the third grade and is to be taught in 40-minute classes, three times a week in the third and fourth grades and four times a week in the fifth and sixth grades and onward (MOE, 2011). (See Appendix 1.1 for an overall description of the standards translated and summarized by Wenfang Fan, one of the book's co-authors.) Toward this end, there are shifts in the way English is to be taught and learned.

The overall shift in the standards aligns with current reforms in Chinese basic education in that they reflect Daoism values embedded in the "integrative child-oriented curriculum" (Huang, 2004, p. 103). In such a curriculum, close attention is paid to the holistic and overall development of students. In this regard, instead of focusing primarily on the acquisition of language skills and knowledge, the new curriculum standards also target students' affective, cognitive, and cross-cultural development. There are now five areas of language development that are targeted in the standards. In addition to students' performance of the four language skills of reading, writing, speaking, and listening and their knowledge of the English language structure (e.g., grammar), the standards also target students' emotional attitude (e.g., motivation), learning strategies, and cultural awareness.

Along with this shift, the standards also reflect a longitudinal and developmental view of language learning. Thus, one significant change is the introduction of English at an earlier grade, that is, the third grade instead of at the middle or junior high school level, as in the past, making English a subject that is taught over a period of nine years instead of just three to four years. This time is needed in order for teachers to develop students in the comprehensive ways previously described. Accordingly, teachers are to use nine levels of English competence to guide their curricular design. From the third grade onward, teachers lead students to reach level 2 in the sixth grade, the end of primary school. At this point, teachers must work to sustain students' interest in learning English, help them develop the ability to greet and exchange information about themselves, their family members and friends, and support their efforts to comprehend and narrate simple stories, to perform easy songs and rhymes, and to participate and cooperate in English learning activities. At the end of the three years at junior middle school, students are expected to reach level 5 where they are confident and motivated in learning English. However, they continue to require teacher assistance to undertake more complex tasks to understand statements about familiar topics and exchange personal opinion, to grasp the main ideas of texts, newspapers, and magazines by means of reading strategies, to draft and revise compositions with the aid of prompts. At this level as well, teachers are to work to develop students' learning strategies and metacognitive skills and in self-assessment.

In the final three years, when the students are at the senior middle/high school levels, they are expected to reach level 7, at which, their teachers should have been able to lead them closer toward being able to undertake English language learning tasks independently. Thus, they should be able to exchange information, pose questions, and express opinions on a wide range of topics, comprehend English literary work in its original form as well as newspapers, and use English functionally such as in writing notices, invitations, and letters. Students should also have the wherewithal to make use of various learning resources and develop individualized learning strategies. At the top two levels of the standards, levels 8 and 9, skills are targeted for autonomous and high ability students who are capable of advancing their English competence in schools with specialized missions such as foreign language studies schools. At these upper levels, students should be able to listen to and understand foreign lectures, seminars, and reports; read general science, technology, and literature articles with the aid of the dictionary; and to write in different genres using available learning resources. Most of all, learners at these levels should ideally be able to seek opportunities to communicate and conduct conversations in English on domestic or international issues, such as environment, population, peace, and development.

It should be noted here that at each of the levels, intercultural awareness is emphasized. Teachers, in this case, are to lead the way in achieving the stated mission of the new standards which is to develop students' ability to adapt and navigate through the demands of "world multi-polarization, economic globalization and informatization" (MOE, 2011, p. 3). The overall shift in the standards as indicated by Zhu (2007, p. 225) is for teachers to "transcend subject centeredness" in their instruction and to guide students instead toward "learning from experience, to know the real world"—a perspective that leans very much toward Daoism.

Another observable trend in the standards is the sustained emphasis on students' ability to use the English language in speaking and writing throughout the nine levels, the instruction of which teachers will have to assume. Lin (2002) specifically points out that the standards are aimed for teachers to guide students to use English productively and as a means for communication. Hence, teachers should "shift from emphasizing the transmission of language knowledge to cultivating students' capabilities in using and practicing the language . . . [instead of] mechanically memorizing it" (Yang, 2012, p. 4). Teachers are to turn to task-based and information-gap types of activities in which problem-solving is core. It is believed that these types of open-end activities where end-points are not pre-determined will lead students to use language more productively and creatively. This emphasis on teachers guiding students' ability to use language in such a way aligns with a related and significant nationwide emphasis on their task to enhance creativity and imagination in students' education (Yang, 2012).

The standards also target students' "good feelings" (感觉良好, ganjue lianghao) toward English language learning as such feelings will affect students' motivation and attitude, a recurring theme in the standards. To achieve these goals, the teacher guide section of the standards encourages teachers not to limit themselves to using only prescribed texts but to include also texts that are rich, diverse, and multi-modal in nature (e.g., video and audio materials as well as the Internet). The teacher guide section also suggests that teachers be aware of and respect students' individual backgrounds, experiences, abilities, and learning styles. One way to achieve this goal is for teachers to use materials from students' lives and from interests they express.

In this regard, Yang (2012) describes teachers as being at the heart of the motivation and creativity of each student. However, given the situation of Chinese classrooms being comparatively large (40–70 students in one class), it is challenging for teachers to be attentive and attuned to each student. Thus, teachers' development of students' ability for self-direction and autonomous learning becomes central in the standards as is their ability to collaborate with others to overcome the difficulties and to accomplish learning tasks (see, for example, standards at levels 4 and 5).

We include the new English language standards in this chapter because they provide an understanding as to the responsibilities that await pre-service teachers when they graduate. In the following section, we take a closer look at curricula from the three major types of teaching training institutions as a means to understand their efforts to get pre-service teachers prepared to assume the responsibilities of guiding their students to meet the standards' expectations.

Curricula Coverage

In this section, we provide a closer look at the curricula that define the educational training of Chinese English language pre-service teachers, at each of the three levels. The curriculum at Beijing Normal University for pre-service teachers bound for high school teaching will be discussed specifically as an example. (For a sample curriculum for normal schools attended by pre-school and kindergarten pre-service teachers see that of Fujian Normal School at www.fjys.edu.cn/Item/1091.aspx. At Hunan First Teacher College's website, a sample curriculum for teacher colleges for junior/middle school teachers can be found at http://dept.hnfnu.edu.cn/fld/News.aspx?bbid=71&nid=10771.)

Table 1.2 provides an overall distribution of courses at the three types of teacher training institution.

Beijing Normal University (BNU) Pre-Service Teacher Training Program

The coursework at the School of Foreign Languages and Literatures for students who are pre-service teachers of English covers a period of four years, at the end of which they receive 156 credit hours toward a Humanities Bachelor degree (文学学士学位, wenxue xueshi xuewei). Students can take seventy courses for 156 credit hours over 160 weeks (see www.sfll.bnu.edu.cn/channels/918.html). (See Table 1.3.)

Indeed, English language courses consist of almost three-fifths of the coursework at 62.2 percent. These courses include courses on English foundation courses and disciplinary foundations. Students can spend up to six of eight semesters taking the courses over the four years that they are in school. They can include a selection of courses such as those on English language skills of reading, listening, writing, speaking, pronunciation, rhetorical styles, public speaking, grammar, linguistics, British and American literature, English language translation strategies, and comparative cultural studies.

TABLE 1.2 Distribution of Pre-Service Teacher Coursework Across Three Institutions

	Credit hours	General courses	Disciplinary courses	% of teacher education courses
Beijing Normal University	156	19.4%	62.2%	18.4%
Hunan First Teacher College	184	27%	36.4%	36.6%
Fujian Normal School	130	26%	36%	38%

TABLE 1.3 BNU's Curriculum

Curriculum type	Courses		Credits
General Course (19.4%)	Ideology and Politics		14
	Information Technology		5
	Physical Education and Health		4
	Military Training and Military theory		2
	Aesthetical Education		2
	University-wide optional course		7
	Total		**34**
Disciplinary Course (62.2%)	Disciplinary Foundations		8
	Disciplinary Foundations		48
	Disciplinary Orientation		34–35
	Total		**90–91**
Teacher Education Course (18.4%)	Teacher Education Foundation	Compulsory Teacher Education Compulsory Course	10
		Educational Research Course	4
		Educational and Teaching Practice	11
	Professional Belief and Nurturing education		2
	Scientific Research and Innovation		0–1
	Thesis Design		4
	Total		**31–32**
总 计(100%)			156

The other significant portion of the curriculum at 19.4 percent are courses focused on the development in pre-service teachers of a sense of responsibility and patriotism to the country. In this regard, the ideology and the military courses serve the purpose. The former course deals with topics on Chinese thinking exemplified by Mao Zedong Thought, Modern History of China while the military coursework covers Chinese territories, its military strength, and achievements of its famous military troops. All students are expected to take the courses as military service is compulsory for young men and women of about 18–19 years of age. The Chinese worldview and appreciation for specific values are covered in the Aesthetics course and include topics such as Chinese Literature Appreciation, painting, sculpture, and other art forms.

Pedagogical courses constitute the last block of courses at 18.4 percent. The compulsory teacher education course covers pedagogical theories and methods including those that involve technology use in teaching. (In the overall picture, they are only about a fifth of the overall coursework in teaching training.) Beliefs about teaching and nurturing is another component of this block. In the educational research course, pre-service teachers are exposed to various types and ways to undertake them. Such knowledge is important as research is also a responsibility teachers have to assume in school. (See Fan's Chapter 4 and Pawan and Fan's Chapter 5.) The largest and most significant component of this block of coursework is teaching practice where teachers are student teaching which takes place over twenty-four weeks. Pre-service teachers' performance in student teaching is weighted most heavily overall and it is a pre-requisite for graduation.

Pre-Service Teacher Experiences

We undertook three focus group interviews on September 19, 2016, with fifteen pre-service teachers (five per group) who are graduates from three institutions at the three levels (normal schools, teacher colleges, and normal university). We used the standards and the curricula as bases for the interviews. From the interviews, we were able to surmise areas of needed improvement as well as existing strengths they saw in the pre-service teacher training programs familiar to them.

From the interviews, the main shortcomings that emerged included that the programs were considered subject-matter heavy, not pedagogically focused, overly theoretical as well as lacking in practice-oriented personnel. This was expressed even by teachers who had graduated from normal schools and teacher colleges which are perceived to be more practice-oriented as institutions. Accordingly, graduates also saw that the programs need to increase their ability to enhance pre-service teachers' English language knowledge and skills as well as their English language pedagogy.

This heavy focus on subject matter knowledge translated into a complaint that it did not transfer into an individual's effectiveness as a teacher, clearly illustrated by this quote:

> Because we had a lot of information from training, now we are very qualified and knowledgeable. But I cannot safely say I can teach.
> *(Shang, teacher college graduate, September 19, 2016)*

The same frustration is reiterated by teacher Hai:

> I do not know how to make the students' learning more effective after I graduated and I still face the problem right now.
> *(Hai, comprehensive normal graduate, September 19, 2016)*

The theoretical nature of the knowledge was also part of the perceived problem:

> We are asked to write thesis or to make public report about the theories we have learnt in the training. Some of the information in the courses were meaningless and I see that now as a teacher in the field.
> *(Ya, normal comprehensive university, September 19, 2016)*

The disjuncture between what is learned in training and actual practice is also related to the types of personnel in teacher training:

> We need people who can teach communication. As a teacher, I need to know how to help students with their communication abilities because they are very important for students to live a better life in society.
> *(Li, normal university graduate, September 19, 2016)*

> Teacher trainers who can help us with the analysis of past papers and testing points should be in our program. That way we can find strategies to support students.
> *(Hsu, comprehensive normal graduate, September 19, 2016)*

Proficiency in the English language also continues to be an elusive skill for the teacher below, despite training:

> The English knowledge system is not well constructed and this was and still is a headache for me. I struggled to understand it during my university life and I still have the same problems even now while I am teaching. I need more and better training.
> *(Wang, normal school graduate, September 19, 2016)*

Finally, another recurring theme that emerged from the interviews is the insufficiency of the training on pre-service teachers' English language pedagogy:

> For me, one of the essential parts is being trained to make an English speech in public. For me, because I was always afraid that I would forget what I wanted to say next while teaching in class. I would write down every word that I would say in class and repeated the words again and again before class. This was not the best way to learn how to teach. I still do not know how to teach the language.
> *(Hong, teacher college graduate, September 19, 2016)*

Despites these worries and laments, the interviewees all agreed that the greatest benefits of their training were derived from teaching practice:

> The most useful part in teaching practice was learning how to plan a lesson and how to take students into consideration when we do lesson preparation. We also saw how lessons worked or did not work when we were practicing.
> *(Zengxiang, teaching college graduate, September 19, 2016)*

> When I was a senior student in the normal school, our teacher let every one of us give a class to our classmates several times. Every time I was

teaching, in my eyes my classmates were like little friends and so I said to them, "If you behave well in my class, I will give you some candies." I saw the bad effect of that immediately as after that my classmates demanded candies from me each time I wanted them to do something. As a result, the last month on campus, I was the poorest student teacher! I know better now.

(Yan, normal school graduate, September 19, 2016)

Going through practice teaching helped me to learn about the real situation in secondary schools. I got to observe and learn how to manage the classroom, which is possibly the most difficult part for a teacher.

(Taozi, normal university graduate, September 19, 2016)

As will be seen in Pei and Jin's Chapter 2, which focuses specifically on the student teaching experience, opportunities to observe and to practice teach give pre-service teachers a grounded sense of what is expected of them, where their abilities lie in terms of the expectations, and the extent to which they should develop their abilities to fulfill the expectations.

Discussions and the Current State of the Situation

Despite the standards calling for a less subject-centric approach, it is clear from views expressed in the previous section and from the curricula especially at institutions that teach students at the upper levels that there is a higher percentage of coursework pertaining to the subject matter. (For example, at BNU, English language courses are at 62.2% and at Hunan First Teacher College, it is 43%.) A strong focus of these programs is to increase pre-service teachers' English language proficiency. In China at this point in time, the acquisition of English mainly depends on the intensive learning within the classroom, given that English is a foreign language and is in a setting where the language is infrequently used outside the classroom. The exposure to the language and the learning opportunities using it are usually confined in the classroom. This reality explains the particular emphasis on English language courses in the programs.

Teacher training institutions' focus on providing pre-service teachers extensive exposure to English language content can also be related to their efforts to overcome the "Deaf and Dumb English" legacy (Kuang & Liu, 2003, p. 118). Public schools have been harshly criticized for not producing students who are able to use the language effectively despite the extended time and exposure to the language. The blame has fallen in particular on the excessive reliance of public school teachers on the Grammar Translation (GT) and Audio-Visual Teaching methods despite calls, evident through the standards described previously, to use more communicative approaches (Kuang & Liu, 2003). (In the GT approach, students are instructed to translate Chinese into English while in the Audio-Visual Teaching approach, the focus is on students' comprehension as they listen to English language input from audio and/or visual sources.) It is a matter of discussion as to what extent the criticism is true but it has also begun to be targeted at the preparation of pre-service teachers in teacher training institutions at the tertiary levels (see Li, 2006).

Confucius's and Laozi's philosophical perspectives on learning through observations and internships with experts shed some light here in terms of the pedagogical training of pre-service teachers. Laozi in particular stresses that teaching is an art in which learning how to do it is less about technical knowledge but is more about understanding how to do it by watching the performance of those who are experts and masters of the craft (see also Fan's Chapter 4). Given this focus it is understandable that pedagogical instruction is shelved until the teachers are in practice or until they are employed in schools. The development of pedagogical expertise is thus reserved until the pre-service teachers can observe senior- and in-service teachers practice in the field. Furthermore, in China, the jiaoyanzu (教研组) system is in place (see Pawan and Fan's Chapter 5), in which new teachers are assigned mentors to guide them in their teaching for as long as they are employed. The mentors provide school-based professional development which is considered in China to be a more relevant and contextualized form of professional development. Admittedly, the sufficiency of this approach continues to be debated.

The disjuncture between theory and practice in teacher training thus described is not confined to the experiences of the interviewees in this study nor to English language teachers in China exclusively. (See, for example, Kumaravadivelu (1994, 2001, 2005, 2006). One reason is the presence of a perspective that the theories and methods that emerge from them are taken as "gospel" in that they are seen as ready to be applied verbatim rather than as guidance to practice. Second- and foreign-language theories are overwhelmingly Western-centric. When they are used in non-Western settings such as in China, they have minimal relevance unless efforts are undertaken to "glocalize" them so that only elements that make sense in the local context are adopted. It is not clear from the curricula and the standards included in this chapter that such efforts are undertaken formally, although informally in classrooms, glocalization is a common practice (Pu & Pawan, 2013). Nevertheless, glocalization of methods is a challenging undertaking as it requires an in-depth understanding of pedagogical theory. Thus, pre-service teachers must be guided and empowered early in their training to "glocalize" approaches to teaching.

The disjuncture of theory and practice can also be related to the problematic set-up of pre-service teacher training in four-year comprehensive universities or normal universities in China. In those institutions, discipline/subject matter and research knowledge are the central focus. Also, courses there are taught by research-oriented professors who are distanced from practice and who receive minimal training themselves to develop their pedagogical skills.

Compounding the problem is that English as a subject matter and the pedagogy that underlies its teaching are taught by different people in different departments. (This problem is also not uncommon in institutions in other countries including the U.S.). More often than not the former is taught in the English and/or Linguistics departments. Pedagogy is taught by professors in the Education Faculty. When this is the case, pre-service teachers find themselves on their own in bridging the knowledge of the subject of English and their understanding of how to teach it. This unnecessary separation leaves pre-service teachers ill prepared.

Through the perspectives we share in this chapter, we are advocating that training institutions provide a balance of subject matter and pedagogical knowledge. In that regard, our attention was drawn to a teacher recruitment effort in May 2016, by a high school affiliated with Renmin University of China. (High-ranking and prestigious public schools are often associated with prestigious Chinese universities.) The sixteen teachers who were offered teaching positions were graduates without teaching degrees but instead were those who had master's and doctoral degrees in their subject areas. (See Renmin University of China, 2016.) Furthermore, besides the three hires who were overseas university graduates, the newly hired teachers were from top universities in China, which, in addition to graduates from Renmin University itself, were from Beijing, Tsinghua, Beijing Foreign Studies universities as well as the Chinese Academy of Science. In this regard, the new teachers' lack of teacher training was overlooked in lieu of their subject matter knowledge (as well as admittedly, their college pedigree).

As discouraging as this may be for teacher educators, the job of educating young and new teachers remains a public service and a societal responsibility that ranks high in the Chinese mindset.

APPENDIX 1.1

Chinese English Language Standards

General Goal Description of the Nine Levels

(Summarized and Translated by Wenfang Fan)

Level 1

The students have curiosity and like hearing others speak English. They can do games, actions, and things (like coloring and matching) according to their teacher's simple instructions. They can do simple role play. They can sing simple English songs and say simple English rhymes. With the help of pictures, they can listen and read to understand simple short stories. They can communicate about their own information, express their feelings and emotions. They can write English letters and words. They are interested in foreign culture and tradition in their learning.

Level 2

The students show their initiative in learning English and have elementary confidence. They can listen to and understand short passages and short stories on familiar topics. They can greet others in English and exchange information about themselves, family, and friends. They can perform short dialogue or rhymes according to what they have learned. They can read to understand short stories and other simple written materials in other styles. They can write simple sentences with the help of examples or pictures. They can participate in simple activities like role play. They can try to use appropriate learning methods to overcome difficulties they run into in their learning. They can realize cultural differences in language communication.

Level 3

The students have interest and elementary confidence in learning English. They can hear and understand some familiar topics and very simple short stories. They can exchange information with their teachers and classmates in the scope of familiar topics (such as school and family life). They can read and understand simple short stories or some other simple written things. They can follow examples or pictures to write some simple sentences. They can participate in simple activities like role play. They can try appropriate learning methods to overcome difficulties they run into in their learning. They can realize cultural differences in language communication.

Level 4

The students are clear about the necessity and the goal of learning English. They show stronger confidence in learning. They can understand conversations in daily life and simple stories. They can exchange information and opinions with their teachers and classmates on topics they are familiar with. They can read and understand short stories. They can write notes and simple letters. They can make use of the different educational resources to get information from audio or written materials, expand their scope of knowledge, solve simple problems and present their solutions. They can help each other overcome difficulties together when they run into difficulties in their learning. They can make appropriate schedules and arrange their learning tasks. They can find out the methods of learning that are suitable for them. They can realize cultural differences in daily language communication and learning.

Level 5

They have the right motivation and the proper attitude toward learning English. They can understand statements on familiar topics the teacher presents and participate in the discussion around the topics. They can exchange information with their teachers and classmates on various topics and present their opinions. They can read and understand the general meanings of simple reading materials, newspapers, and magazines designed for seventh to ninth graders in spite of some new words. They can adopt different reading strategies according to the goals of their reading. They can write and modify simple essays according to hints provided. They can cooperate with others to solve problems, present their solutions, and complete learning tasks. They can evaluate their own study and summarize some leaning methods. They make use of the various educational resources to help themselves with their learning. They can have a better understanding of cultural differences.

Level 6

The students can have stronger motivation and awareness of learning English on their own initiative. They can understand points of view in both audio and written materials and express their own opinion on them. They can describe their own experiences properly with oral or written language. They can plan, organize, and implement learning activities with the help of their teachers. They can make use of the educational resources on a wider scope and get information from various resources. They can evaluate their study and adjust goals and strategies of learning accordingly. They can realize the cultural background embodied by language and communication.

Level 7

The students will have durative learning motivation and the awareness of learning on their own initiative. They can exchange information on various topics, ask questions, and present their own opinions and suggestions. They can read and understand simplified English original works and English magazines and newspapers designed for high school students. They are able to write practical essays, such as notes and invitation letters. Under the teacher's guidance, they can plan, organize, and implement various language practice activities. They can make use of various educational resources to help with their learning. They can have the initial ability to direct themselves and form their own learning strategies. They can understand cultural differences in communication and form an initial awareness of cross-cultural communication.

Level 8

The students can have strong confidence in learning English and the ability to learn on their own initiative. They can talk fluently with native English speakers on familiar topics. They can give their evaluative opinions on ideas presented in audio or written form. They can write coherent short essays with good structure. They can plan, organize, and implement various language practice activities, such as discussing and making plans and reporting the results of experiments and surveys all by themselves. They can make use of various educational resources, such as the Internet, to obtain and process information. They can evaluate their study achievement and form effective learning strategies. They can understand the different cultural backgrounds embodied in communications and learn to understand and respect other nations' culture.

Level 9

They are able to learn on their own initiative. They can understand speeches, discussions, debates, and reports about familiar topics. They can talk about hot topics, such as environment protection, population, peace, and development in English and are able to present their own attitudes and opinions. They can do interpretation on occasions of daily communication. They can communicate in English in real communication events. They can read articles of popular science and literary works with the aid of a dictionary. They can write common practical essays and have the initial ability to make use of literature. They are able explore study resources on their own, in order to enrich their study resources. They will have a clear awareness that the world is a big family.

References

Huang, F. (2004). Curriculum reform in contemporary China: Seven goals and six strategies. *Journal of Curriculum Studies, 36*(1), 101–105.

Kuang, Ch., & Liu, L. (2003). Viewing the listening and spoken language teaching of college English teaching from the phenomenon of "deaf and dumb" style English. *Journal of Harbin University, 24*(10), 118–119.

Kumaravadivelu, B. (1994). The postmethod condition: (E)merging strategies for second/foreign language teaching. *TESOL Quarterly, 28*(1), 27–48.

Kumaravadivelu, B. (2001). Toward a postmethod pedagogy. *TESOL Quarterly, 35*(4), 537–560.

Kumaravadivelu, B. (2005). In defence of postmethod. *ILI Language Teaching Journal, 1*(1), 15–19.

Kumaravadivelu, B. (2006). *Understanding language teaching: From method to postmethod.* Mahwah, NJ: Lawrence Erlbaum.

Li, B. (2006, November 26). *Premier Wen Jiabao seeks advice from university presidents on how to prepare excellent talents.* Retrieved from http://news.xinhuanet.com/school/2006-11/28/content_5400168.htm

Lin, L. (2002). English education in present-day China. *Asian/Pacific Book Development, 33*(2), 8–9.

Ministry of Education. (2011). *English curriculum standards for full-time compulsory education* (Edited Version). Beijing: People's Republic of China. Retrieved from www.moe.gov.cn/srcsite/A26/s8001/201112/t20111228_167340.html

Pu, H., & Pawan, F. (2013). *The pedagogy and practice of Western-educated Chinese English language teachers: Foreign education, Chinese meanings.* New York: Routledge.

Ren Min University of China. (2016, May 24). *Teacher's office: New teacher recruitment for attachment middle school of Ren Min University.* [EB/OL]. Retrieved from http://hr.ruc.edu.cn/displaynews.php?id=10549

Yang, X. R. (2012). Using English to do things: Capabilities-oriented amendments of the English curriculum standards: Working group interviews in amending the English curriculum standards ["Yong Yingyu Zuoshi": Nengli Daoxiang de Yingyu Kecheng Biaozhun Xiuding—Zhuangfang Yiwu Jiaoyu Yingyu Kecheng Biaozhun Xiuding Gongzuozu]. *Jiangsu Education Reseach, 5C,* 4–7.

Yao, F. Q., & Chen, S. J. (2009). On professional commitment of tuition free normal university students. *Contemporary Teacher Education*, *2*(1), 62–67.

Zhu, M. (2007). Recent Chinese experiences in curriculum reform. *Prospects*, *37*(2), 223–235.

Zhu, X. D. (2015). On the three track multi-level system of teacher education in China. *Teacher Education Research*, *27*(6), 1–7.

2
STUDENT TEACHING
"All the Sour, Sweet, Bitter, and Pungent Flavors Must Be Tested"

Miao Pei and Wei Jin

Introduction

The student teaching (教育实习, jiaoyu shixi) experience consists of approximately 12 percent of students' overall training, a small percentage of their overall teacher preparation experience. However, students cannot graduate if they underperform in the student teaching experience. It is thus an essential component to their training because of three reasons: the experience is an opportunity to link theory and practice; to learn how to apply their content knowledge to real life circumstances in the classroom (Yao, Li & Zhang, 2012); and finally, as a means for pre-service teachers to showcase their abilities to people who may play critical roles in their future employment (Hu, 1987; Qin & Zhou, 2001).

The student teaching experience runs counter to traditional beliefs that knowledge is the sole foundation of expertise (Shen & Li, 2001; Chen, 2003; Wang, 2003). The student teaching requirement clearly demonstrates the view that one part of the expertise is to be derived from immersing pre-service teachers (known also as student teachers in this chapter) in classroom-based experiences. The experience not only shapes the teachers' conceptualization of what they can do but also who they will be as professionals in the future, in ways that will be illustrated in three cases at the end of the chapter.

Student Teaching Models

There are three Chinese student teaching models in place. First is the "traditional model" in which student-teaching internships begin toward the end of pre-service teachers' undergraduate experience. In this model, student teaching takes place in their seventh semester before the eighth and final semester of their studies. During this time, the pre-service teachers are usually at their student-teaching sites for 3 months or so, depending on the need of the schools to which they are assigned or of the provinces in which the schools are located.

In a variation of the same model described in the previous paragraph, the "teacher replacement" model (顶岗实习, dinggang shixi) is specifically designed for student teaching experiences in the rural areas (Wang & Feng, 2015, p. 91). (See also Pei and Jin's Chapter 7.) In this model, pre-service teachers are assigned to relieve teachers in the areas to provide the latter time to pursue teacher training in universities. In this regard, the pre-service teachers become teacher substitutes for a short period of time of about a month or less. This experience can be added on to the regular student-teaching experience or it can be an extension of the experience. In another variation of this model, pre-service teachers are specifically assigned to student teach in specific rural areas for the entirety of the 3-month experience because there is a shortage of teachers in those areas. As described in Chapter 7, such arrangements are in place particularly in the western, mountainous, and ethnically diverse regions of China such as Guizhou, Ningxia, and Xinjiang provinces.

A new and emerging model is the Consecutive Model (连续模式, lianxu moshi). In this model which is implemented in Beijing Municipality and Hubei Province, pre-service teachers are placed in student-teaching sites several times during their undergraduate training, so that they can see immediately how theory they learn in universities is put into practice as well as understand and engage in the adaptation and modifications of both. In Beijing United Normal University, one of the institutions where this model is used, in their freshman year, pre-service teachers observe classes in schools; in the second and third years (in the second and sixth semesters), they undertake what is known as "imitation" teaching where they replicate the teaching they observed; in the seventh semester of the fourth year, students undertake "real" internships where they student teach, and in the eighth and final semester, they undertake research on their experience (Center for Teacher Education, 2016). The approach in this model is undertaken as it is considered that postponing the student-teaching experience until toward the end of the pre-service teachers' studies is too late. By this time, theoretical ideas become too remote and teaching practice too devoid of context.

In recent years, a new model has emerged and been labeled as a "program-based" student-teaching experience. In this model, universities partner up with schools to identify problems in the schools that pre-service teachers could be assigned to study and to help resolve. (One such partnership is between Beijing Normal University and Jiangbei District of Chongqing which has existed since 2014.) The thinking behind this model is that the pre-service teachers can gain invaluable insight into the inner workings of schools while working on the problems, in addition to learning how to teach. The problems are to be identified onsite and can range from micro issues such as materials used in schools to macro-level issues such as community services.

These models provide an overarching framework as to how student teaching is undertaken. Each teaching training institution will have modifications to each of the models in ways that are most workable in their circumstances.

The Process

Across all the student-teaching models, there are well-defined stages to be completed. In order, these stages include the teaching site assignment, observations, reflections on observations, and teaching demonstration.

Depending on the models used by their institutions, pre-service teachers are assigned to different sites at different times. There is governmental financial assistance for lodgings and transport for the pre-service teachers but the amount differs depending on specific localities to which they are assigned. Be that as it may, the pre-service teachers are assigned to cooperating schools in urban and/or rural areas, in close proximity to their training institutions or to provinces far away. For example, Beijing Normal University (BNU) sends its pre-service teachers to Tianjin city or to Hebei and Shanxi provinces, all of which are close to Beijing. The teachers can also be sent to schools in the northwest territory such as in Ningxia, Gansu, and Xinjiang, to the southwest such as to Yunnan and Guizhou provinces, and to the southeast such as in the provinces of Shandong, Anhui, and Jiangsu.

Pre-service teachers are assigned in groups of ten to twelve to a certain school. They are in a cohort system to enable them to serve as peer-mentors to each other as they go through the experience together. At their assigned schools, the pre-service teachers are assigned to classroom teachers who, in turn, have multiple responsibilities toward them. Besides supervising pre-service teachers' learning and maintaining communications with their teacher training institutions, the host teachers also have to oversee food and lodging and other arrangements to ensure the pre-service teachers' personal comfort.

Regardless of the institutions that they are from and the training they received there, pre-service teachers will be given new training that is specific to the cooperating schools to which they've been assigned to student teach. Orientation meetings are held when the pre-service teachers arrive at the schools, and that can be for two to three days or more, depending on the circumstances of each school. Generally, during this time, experienced teachers in the schools introduce the pre-service teachers to information about the school culture, rules, and regulations. The former will demonstrate education theories they subscribe to and well-known teacher educators that they are informed by. In addition, the experienced teachers from the schools provide demonstration classes to illustrate how they teach and manage students.

Pre-service teachers are then assigned in groups of two to five people to different grade levels and are given specific instructions to complete two central tasks. First, they are to experience to the fullest the rhythm of the schooling life of the students and the people who teach them. They are expected to live with the students in dormitories (when this is applicable) and engage in curricular activities such as in sports or in special interest associations. They must know, understand, and abide by the rules and regulations that affect their students as well as their cooperating teachers. If they see any transgression to the rules, they have the obligation to report to the school's principal or other officials and in this circumstance, they also serve as responsible members of the school staff rather than mere passive observers.

The second and equally important task for pre-service teachers on student-teaching assignments is to observe and learn pedagogy from their cooperating teacher mentors. They are expected to reflect on the notes they take on effective teaching and classroom management approaches as well as problems that are specific to classrooms in the areas in which they teach, particularly if they are in impoverished and ethnically diverse areas of the country. These reflections are to be discussed with their teacher mentors who then report the outcomes of the reflection sessions to the pre-service teachers' university supervisors.

This observation and reflection period can last up to 3 months, depending on the cooperating teachers' estimation of the pre-service teachers' readiness and the specific circumstances of the schools.

Student-Teaching Demonstration Classes

At the end of the observation and reflection periods, pre-service teachers will then be instructed to develop a lesson plan and to demonstrate how to teach from it. The 45-minute demonstration period at the end of the student-teaching experience is probably the most anxiety-filled component of the pre-service teachers' experience in the field. They are to demonstrate their teaching abilities in front of a large audience of students, all the teachers in the school who teach their subject (which in this case is English), and of course, in the presence of peers in their student-teaching cohort. Besides providing the pre-service teachers with an opportunity to showcase what they have learned, the format of these demonstration sessions is also to replicate the experience of teachers participating in competitions, an experience that will define the pre-service teachers' lives once they are employed as they gain full-time status (see Pawan's Chapter 6).

The success of pre-service teachers in teaching lessons at these demonstration sessions depends on multiple factors that precede the public delivery of the lessons. First, it depends on the mentors they are assigned to and who guide and support them throughout the preparation process. The mentors can be the pre-service teachers' cooperating teachers or other empathetic teachers whose schedules allow them time to be mentors. Second, success depends on the pre-service teachers having cohort members capable of providing useful input and advice that enable them to make adjustments to their lesson plans and to their teaching. Third, and most important of all, is the pre-service teachers' effectiveness in using information from the teaching practice they observed in their lesson planning and delivery. The entire process of lesson preparation can take the pre-service teachers as long as a month or even more. The evaluation of their demonstration teaching sessions is based generally on subject area knowledge, extensiveness of lesson planning, quality and use of teaching materials, delivery of the lesson, initiation and sustainment of classroom interaction, evaluation of students, and homework design and assignment. The evaluation criteria are often similar to those used in teaching competitions (see Pawan's Chapter 6).

The student-teaching life for pre-service teachers is vastly different from their experiences as college students, where they can get away with sitting in the back and passively listening to lectures, if they choose to do so. Instead, just like regular teachers, the pre-service teachers are expected to actively assume teaching responsibilities and are challenged to engage daily with students. The student-teaching experience is thus a challenging time but it is also a very formative time for pre-service teachers.

Individual Case Studies of Student-Teaching Experiences

To gain deeper insight into the student-teaching experience and what it could be like for individual pre-service teachers, we include here three case studies derived from the reflective writing of pre-service teachers under our supervision. As mentioned previously, the student-teaching experience is not easy and is filled with experiences that are sweet, sour, and bitter, but they are all pungent and necessary in the training of pre-service teachers. Pre-service teacher experiences in each of the case studies demonstrate several of these "flavors." Pseudonyms are used throughout the three cases.

Dissonance Between Ideal Expectations and Reality: The Case of Mozhi

For Mozhi, whom we interviewed on September 12, 2016, her student-teaching experience is a case of dissonance between what she had envisioned teaching and her role as a teacher to be and what they turned out to be in reality. Both of Mozhi's parents were professors in military and civilian colleges and thus were busy professionals. Because of the nature of her parents' job, Mozhi grew up to be a disciplined and ambitious individual. Her father had strict rules of behavior in the house in which every member was expected to do their work judiciously and to be respectful in private and in public. Through her mother's connections on her job, Mozhi came into contact with her mother's colleagues and could see, through their successes, many possibilities waiting for her in the future.

Mozhi's solid foundation at home gave her a strong platform to excel in school. In primary school, she demonstrated academic excellence as well as a special versatility in the arts and in performance. She was often enlisted to play musical instruments (piano and Guqin, a traditional Chinese musical instrument) and sing and dance in school ceremonies. In secondary school, she demonstrated sensitivity and talent as a writer. She produced highly regarded essays which won competitions and were published in magazines. University life was an equally rewarding experience for Mozhi during which she majored in language and literature. Besides putting in hard work toward her studies, she was able to pursue interests in painting, playing the clavichord, reading widely as well as availing herself of the opportunity to attend lectures by famous professors.

Clearly, Mozhi felt fulfilled with her public school and university experiences. She came out of it confident and very sure of herself:

> I swam like a fish in water in school and at university. I went through my school and university life experience smoothly. I have a lot of papers that won prizes on my wall and I know my teachers are very proud of me.

As she approached graduation as an undergraduate, Mozhi began thinking about becoming a teacher. She enrolled in Beijing Normal University's "4 + 2" program which enabled her to add 2 more years of teacher training coursework to her 4-year undergraduate degree. Mozhi did so as she was inspired particularly by her father:

> I wanted to be a teacher to follow my father's footsteps. I wanted to be able to be of service to the community.

She started courses in teacher education, including pedagogy, educational history, and educational thoughts. However, she was disappointed in the courses because she felt they did not provide her the knowledge she needed to be a teacher:

> The professors fully taught us about educational history, about important educators and their education theories. But I felt that the things we learned in class was far away from real situations in primary and secondary schools.

Upon completion of those courses, Mozhi became part of a cohort of pre-service teachers who traveled together to undertake student teaching in a primary school in Beijing. In the cohort group, she was discouraged to hear from several of her peers that they did not have a good opinion of teaching and wondered why they were going into teaching in the first place. Mozhi was particularly worried when she heard them suggest that teaching meant an end point of a career, especially when she heard the following from one of her peers:

> Being a teacher means a perished life in the future.

Mozhi's disappointment with her teacher education classes and the worry that developed from hearing some of her classmates' views were the beginning of the dissonance and uneasiness that Mozhi was feeling toward teaching. Unfortunately, her student-teaching experiences only served to confirm both feelings.

In the first month of her internship, Mozhi spent much of the time observing her cooperating teacher's classroom at the fourth grade level. Two experiences stood out in her mind:

> When I went into the student-teaching experience, I was hoping that as a teacher, I could lead my students to experience the beauty of language and literature. But all I saw everyday was grammar teaching. The class was also noisy and the students were too naughty to be taught.

Several of the students who were misbehaving also quarreled with the classroom teacher. What she saw frightened Mozhi and crushed her idealistic view of a teacher being someone kind and understanding:

> The female teacher was shouting at the students and said that they were not smart enough. The teacher got into such a fury that she even kicked the students. I was a bit scared.

These experiences in student teaching clearly did not align with the ideals that Mozhi had as to what teaching and being a teacher should be. Consequently, Mozhi decided not to be a classroom teacher. It is a shame, as Mozhi had great potential to be a capable teacher given her background and educational history.

Being Open to Learning With Others: The Case of Chenxuan

In Chenxuan's story, the student-teaching experience enabled her to grow and blossom as a person and as a teacher. It created space for her to develop and form understandings through her interactions with others. On September 30, 2016, she shared with us her 2012 student-teaching experiences.

Chenxuan's family background is quite different from Mozhi. Growing up, her parents were both doctors who took a hands-off approach to parenting and encouraged her to pursue her own interests. She described herself as a free-spirited person who did not always do well in school. She struggled in primary school and fell behind. In secondary school, English was a subject that she was most frustrated with, particularly with its grammatical structures and mechanics of writing. However, she enjoyed reading in English and indulged in it extensively. Chenxuan found ways to befriend teachers whom she liked and to stay away from those she felt were too strict and demanding. This was the same way she maneuvered herself amongst peers and friends alike. Despite her struggles with academics and deliberate efforts she had to put into relationship building, Chenxuan felt her life in school was a good experience for her and made her curious about the world. The teaching profession, she felt, was a way to continue to explore and learn as an individual.

Chenxuan, unlike Mozhi who spent much of her student-teaching time observing, was immediately assigned to teach a class. Her students' journal entries allowed her to see for the first time how she was being perceived as a teacher. She recalled a journal entry by one of her students about her:

> . . . the teacher is medium-built, nothing special. However, I think that she is the most excellent "practice" teacher I have ever met. She stirs up discussion in the classroom. She reads the book with fresh eyes. That is because she has read many other books.
> *(Chenxuan's student, September 18, 2012)*

In addition, instead of passively observing, Chenxuan also sought the help and counsel of her mentor teachers upon realizing immediately from the very beginning she had limited knowledge on what and how to teach:

> I gradually learned to go to master teachers and asked them to check whether I identified correctly the important points to teach students. The experienced teachers were always very nice to me. Also, I began to learn from them about what the students did not understand in class. I occasionally took this information as the content I should pay special attention to during my class.

Chenxuan also engaged with students beyond the classroom for opportunities that enabled her to understand and connect with students:

> I went shopping with my students often. I like to listen to them talk. They often share stories about something that happened to them or something they saw. I sometimes use the stories in my lessons as a way to keep them interested and to let them know I know them.

To further engage students, Chenxuan also drew on her special talents:

> I am good at playing Ping Pong and I occasionally played it with one or two students. Several of them started inviting me to join them in a game

or two. Also, several students and I worked on English cross-word puzzles which I like.

At the end of it all, Chenxuan felt that her efforts to be a good teacher were recognized by students. For example, on her birthday, she was pleasantly surprised to find the following waiting for her in the teachers' office:

> . . . [A] bundle of flowers and chocolates on my table in the office! I was most happy when I saw on the cards that were there, that the students had written the word, "Teacher" next to my name. I realized that students saw me as a real teacher. That made me really happy and increased my confidence in myself.

In Chenxuan's case, we saw that her student-teaching experience, instead of scaring her like it did Mozhi, provided her with an opportunity to grow into the profession and to learn about what she was capable of. Her openness and willingness to venture out and engage with her mentor teachers as well as her students enabled her to learn about components of teaching in the real world that she was curious about and gave her confidence that she will be a successful teacher in the near future.

Carrying Over Persistency and Work Ethic Into Teaching: The Case of Taotao

Taotao was a pre-service teacher from a rural area in the central part of China. Both of Taotao's parents were farmers who worked very hard to earn money to support Taotao's education. Fortunately, Taotao was a good student at the university. However, the struggles of his parents were always on his mind and were in the background of his experiences as a pre-service teacher. We interviewed him on October 10, 2016.

Taotao was eager to begin his student teaching because he knew how much a teacher could influence students and make them feel good about themselves, despite their circumstances. He provided an example from his middle school years:

> My geography teacher asked my class which country was the largest cotton producer in the world behind China and the U.S. My classmates all were very quiet. She then looked at me and said that because I was a farmer's son, I might be able to help us all with the answer. I mentioned the climate, source of water and a few other things. From the information, I helped my classmates deduce that Uzbekistan was the country. My teacher praised me and this left me with a very lasting good impression.

To become a teacher, Taotao studied in a provincial teachers' college and worked very hard during his four years there. He read nearly all the 300 books assigned during those years. Also, while in school, to help pay for his education which his family could not afford, he taught English classes in a training school during weekends and vacations.

During his seventh semester, Taotao was assigned to student teach in a school which was located in the same city as the teachers' college where he was studying and being trained as a teacher. He considered himself to be very fortunate because this enabled him to continue to work to teach English on the side and thus to continue to supplement his own income as well as that of his parents'. Needless to say that throughout his student-teaching experience, his family's circumstances and his work experiences shaped his view as a pre-service teacher. He believed in hard work as a means to success for himself and his students:

> I volunteered to tutor a female student daily because her academic performance was not good. Every day, I would teach her over and over again sentence patterns but she would never get them. But I did not give up. Just like my geography teacher, I let her know that I have seen that she had abilities in other skills and that she was capable of doing great things when she tried hard.

He came about this information when he walked into her singing in an auditorium:

> I was absorbed by her beautiful voice. After the performance, I praised her and her eyes lit up and [she] said to me proudly that she was able to sing the song only after multiple practices.

Taotao also worked hard to improve his teaching. Just like Chenxuan, he used his after-school hours to find ways to connect with students:

> I was assigned to observe fourth and eighth grade classes for a week. But they were taught in the traditional ways where teachers kept talking the entire time. Students lost interest almost immediately. I wanted to make a change to this. So to prepare for my own class, I took pictures of my students inside and outside the classroom and used them in my teaching. I was very happy that the students were very astonished when they saw the pictures. From the first day, I felt I had a good connection with them and got them immediately talking with me.

Taotao also reported working hard in other ways, most particularly in reflecting constantly about his teaching. He kept a diary of his teaching practices, a leftover of his practice of keeping a diary since his middle school days:

> Whenever I could spare some time, which was never enough, I reviewed my diary. I could not believe that I had written down such great thoughts

about a common situation in school life. I could not believe that at that time, for example that I could tell what the students were thinking from facial expressions.

Clearly from these examples, Taotao has emerged as a thoughtful and responsible teacher. His work ethic during his student-teaching days was exemplary and given his background, the ethic will undoubtedly carry over into his career as a full-fledged and responsible English teacher.

Pulling It All Together

The three cases in this chapter demonstrate that the student-teaching experience, despite all educational intents and purposes, translates differently where individual learnings are concerned. What the experiences show us is that pre-service teachers' backgrounds could have an effect on the way they approach student teaching and what they derive from the experience. The pre-service teachers' expectations as students also came into play. For Mozhi, she expected an alignment between her expectations with what she found in reality; for Chenxuan, it was the "uncovery" of information yet unknown to her but that she was curious to know about; and for Taotao, it was the fulfillment of his belief in hard work and the ability of teachers to make a difference in the lives of others.

As to teacher identity outcomes, Tan (2012) concluded that pre-service teachers' identity formation as a teacher is greatly influenced by the people with whom they come into contact during student teaching. If their own expectations align with their experiences, the pre-service teachers' initial conception of their identity is enhanced; if not, they are likely to change or transform it into something else. This is certainly true in the case of Mozhi where the people she came into contact with served to solidify her uneasiness about being a teacher and this convinced her to leave the professional pursuit of it altogether. For Chenxuan, the people she encountered in her student-teaching experience helped her to understand herself better as a teacher and what she could do using her own agency. For Taotao, his student-teaching encounters confirmed in him what he knew to be true of himself and what he knew would make him a great teacher.

In undertaking these case studies, we also see the power of reflection as a means for each of the three student teachers we interviewed to learn about themselves. (See, for example, Korthagen, 1985; Zeichner & Liston, 2013.) A most significant study that confirmed this position for Chinese educators was undertaken by Huang and Zhang (2015) describing the types of information that student teachers reflect on. The respondents in this research were those who majored in English ($n = 240$) from province-level normal universities. Overall, the central focus of their reflections focused on issues of morality, feelings toward their students, thinking about their thinking (meta-cognition), and about their practice. At the lower end of the spectrum are reflections on regulations. However, student teachers have to be taught or guided to reflect or otherwise they will concentrate primarily on the mechanics of instruction (Han & Wang, 2008; Lan & Zhang, 2009). This is confirmed by Pawan and Fan's study described in Chapter 5.

Conclusion: Tensions That Remain

As we write this chapter and think about the experiences of the pre-service students we supervise, we continue to think about tensions that remain unarticulated by these pre-service teachers. First, we see that there is a disjuncture between the type of training that student teachers receive in their teacher training institutions and the realities on the ground. This disjuncture was discussed in Chapter 1 by Pei, Pawan, and Jin. We also are concerned about the imposition that schools complain about when they host student teachers. Primary and secondary school teachers in China fear that when they give up class time for pre-service teachers to practice, they are taking time away from preparing their students for high-stakes examinations such as the gaokao. As mentioned in Chapter 7 (Pei and Jin) and Chapter 8 (Wang), there is also tension from the insecurity about pre-service teachers' ability to provide qualified guidance to students.

We are also aware of the need to train the cooperating teachers in how to support and to guide the pre-service teachers undertaking the student-teaching experience. Negativity and/or top-down guidance can discourage pre-service teachers and constrain their ability to try out new ideas (see also Pawan and Fan's Chapter 5). We are aware how this limited experience can influence pre-service teachers for a lifetime (Guo & Wang, 2009) and fossilize unnecessarily ideas that need to be changed. Once ideas are implanted in the minds of new teachers, it may take constant guidance to help them see and be open to alternative ways of instruction.

The student-teaching experience for Chinese pre-service teachers culminates in a demonstration teaching for which they have to practice multiple times and can often be the sole focus of the student-teaching experience at the expense of everything else that the pre-service teachers are experiencing. Similar to Pawan's criticism of the competitions (see Chapter 6), student teachers are primarily focused on performing rather than actual teaching.

Finally, we also empathize with our pre-service teachers who find themselves in a status limbo in their student-teaching experience. They are in an insecure situation as individuals who have yet to graduate from their teacher training institutions, as trainees who are subject to the discretion of classroom teachers, and as temporary teachers who do not have real authority over the students they teach. It is a difficult and vulnerable place to be for anyone but especially for young teachers.

References

Center for Teacher Education. (2016). *A report on teacher education in China*. (Unpublished report). Beijing Normal University, Beijing, China.

Chen, X. M. (2003). Practical knowledge: Knowledge base for teacher professional development. *Peking University Education Review, 1*(1), 104–112.

Gall, M. D., Gall, J. P., & Borg, W. R. (2007). *Educational research: An introduction* (8th ed.). Boston: Pearson.

Guo, X. J., & Wang, Q. (2009). An exploration of relationship between educational internship and English student teachers' professional development. *Foreign Languages and Their Teaching, 3*, 28–33.

Han, G., & Wang, R. (2008). On understanding of reflective practice of pre-service teachers. *Foreign Language Teaching Theory and Practice, 3*, 82–87.

Hu, Er. G. (1987). An initial exploration of role theories and student-teacher relationship. *Educational Theory and Practice, 6*, 36–39.

Huang, H., & Zhang, W. R. (2015). Status quo of reflection from English majors in normal institute. *Education Research Monthly, 4*, 69–74.

Korthagen, F. A. (1985). Reflective teaching and pre-service teacher education in the Netherlands. *Journal of Teacher Education, 36*(5), 11–15.

Lan, Y., & Zhang, B. (2009). Reflective competence training of pre-service teachers in UK. *Comparative Competence Review, 12*, 11–15.

Qin, Q. W., & Zhou, Y. H. (2001). *An introduction of role theory*. Beijing: China Social Science Press.

Shen, J. L., & Li, Q. (2001). Curriculum reform in perspective of primary and secondary teachers' knowledge status. *Curriculum, Teaching Materials, and Teaching Methods, 21*(11), 49.

Tan, H. W. (2012). *From the perspective of significant others to see student teachers' professional identity formation—a narrative of a student teacher*. (Unpublished thesis). Beijing Normal University, Beijing, China.

Wang, B. S., & Feng, Y. H. (2015). Difficulties and solutions in implementation of the "Guo Pei Plan." *China Educational Journal, 2015*(10), 88–92.

Wang, C. S. (2003). A critical reflection on the thought of "despising knowledge" in Chinese Basic Education. *Peking University Education Review, 2*(3), 5–23.

Yao, Y., Li, F. H., & Zhang, J. H. (2012). Reflection on the reform routes of normal students in educational practice in China. *Educational Research, 385*(2), 103–108.

Yin, R. (1989). *Case study research*. Thousand Oaks, CA: Sage.

Zeichner, K. M., & Liston, D. P. (2013). *Reflective teaching: An introduction*. New York: Routledge.

3
PERMANENT TEACHER QUALIFICATIONS

"Surviving Within the Iron Rice Bowl"

Wenfang Fan, Ge Wang, and Xin Chen

Introduction

"Iron Rice Bowl" is a metaphoric term symbolizing jobs in which there are stable income and benefits for employees. In particular, these are jobs which are directly connected to the central government and state-run enterprises including the civil service. They also encompass teaching positions in government-run public schools. Such jobs are considered secure in their longevity and are accompanied with benefits such as free housing, education, and medical service. This was the case before the 1990s when China's economy was centrally planned and controlled in which, besides setting economic goals, policies, investments and prices, the government also allocated and distributed resources. However, the situation is quite different at this point in time. Because there is an increasing number of students graduating from universities, the government can no longer promise civil-service employment for everyone. The current unemployment rate for graduates, 6 months after they leave college, is at 15 percent, that is, approximately 1 million individuals (Silbert, 2014). Furthermore, because the market economy now prevails in the country, the private sector creates more opportunities and competition that draw away many talented and ambitious young people from state-owned enterprises. There are thus fewer permanent jobs to be had and within this context, the job as a teacher is highly valued. However, job candidates must meet requirements to demonstrate compliancy to the system in order to the qualify for the job. This chapter discusses the factors that come into consideration when individuals strive to do so in order to be teachers who are permanent employees of the Chinese government.

Getting Into and Staying in the Iron Bowl

As was described in Pei, Pawan, and Jin's Chapter 1, until recently individuals who graduated from normal schools, teaching colleges, and universities were qualified to be permanent teachers. However, currently all graduates aspiring to be teachers also have to be certified through examinations. Once certified, teachers are permanently employed as is stated in the Ministry of Education (2001) document entitled *Guided Principles on Issues Concerning the First-time Teacher Certification*.

The certification process that enables teachers to hold permanent positions began in 2011; Zhejiang and Hubei provinces were picked as "experimental provinces" for the teacher certification examinations run by the Ministry of Education. Other provinces such as Guangxi, Hainan, Shandong, and Anhui as well as influential cities such as Beijing and Shanghai, followed suit. In 2015, all provinces in China, with the exceptions of Hong Kong, Tai Wan, and Macao, adopted the certification examination. The Ministry of Education administers the written portion of the examination while officials in local governments undertake oral interviews.

The written examination involves teachers' knowledge of two subjects, namely, knowledge of pedagogy and educational psychology. The examinations are held twice a year in the spring and fall and can be taken as many times as needed until teachers pass both subjects to obtain their certificates. The maximum points to be scored for each subject is 150 points and although the MOE can make changes, the passing score is usually 70 points. Interviews, on the other hand, focus on teachers' ability to respond to the local officials' questions on how they could problem solve specific teaching challenges such as parental complaints and teaching strategies for specific types of content. At the end of it all, teachers who are successful in the written and oral examinations obtain certificates that are valid nationwide. From 2015 onward, teachers must reapply for renewal of their teacher certificate every five years. In this new requirement, the renewal of the certificates is based on annual appraisals of teachers' good ethical behavior and their participation in teacher training of no less than 360 hours over five years.

Admittedly, this new certification and renewal policy makes it more challenging for Chinese teachers to become a teacher. Nevertheless, once they are certified, they have a secure position with the government. They are given multiple opportunities to renew their certificates in the ways previously described and in that regard, their teaching position, once obtained, is permanent.

The Teaching Load

Although there are variations in the number of teaching hours, generally, the numbers range from 14–18 periods a week for elementary, twelve to fifteen hours a week for middle/junior high school, and ten to thirteen hours a week for senior high school teachers. Each period is about 40–45 minutes long. However, the number of hours in the classroom does not fully reflect the responsibilities of a classroom teacher. The teaching profession in China is considered a "hardship" profession (辛苦, xinku). This is not only because of teachers' extensive responsibilities in large classrooms (40 students in classrooms in big cities and 70 in under-resourced schools), they also have extensive responsibilities that extend beyond the classroom. (See also Pawan and Fan's Chapter 5.)

Although the school day starts at eight in the morning and ends at five in the evening, Chinese public school teachers have to arrive at school not later than 7:30 a.m. The time between 7:30 a.m. to 8:00 a.m. is used for morning reading of Chinese and English texts. Thus, teachers of both subjects spend the early morning hours supervising students in their reading or reciting of texts in the two languages. For each of the 40- to 45-minute classes taught, teachers are expected to spend anywhere from two to three hours to prepare lessons, and for new teachers their preparation time may take twice as long. Each day homework has to be assigned and graded to reinforce students' learning and to prepare them for upcoming tests and examinations, a process that can take twice as much time as classroom teaching. Homeroom teachers only teach two classes (i.e. 10 hours per week) but they supervise daily morning (second period) and afternoon (sixth period) exercises and students' naptime; organize spring and fall field trips, holiday celebrations, and competitions in various skills (e.g., reading, singing, calligraphy).

Chinese public schools are known for their extended break time (noon to 2 p.m.) which includes lunch that is provided by the school as well as naptime for everyone from elementary to high school. In schools, there are individual cots for teachers to rest in. However, during this time, teachers also meet individually with students. After school is over, teachers stay back to tutor students who are falling behind or to provide extra classes because they feel those classes are needed to improve a student's individual performance or that of the entire class or even for the grade level as a whole. Teachers come back to school to work with students until late in the evening for these extra classes and it is not uncommon that both students and teachers return home at nine or ten in the evening. Many also offer themselves over the weekend to tutor students voluntarily or to be paid to do so.

Pawan and Fan in Chapter 5 also describe teachers' involvement in their students' lives that go beyond meeting with parents and contacting them when problems occur in school. They point out that because they are with students for an extended length of time, they also feel that they play the role of surrogate parents to their students, often staying with them at school when no one is at home. This is especially the case in big cities where both parents are often busy at work.

Another significant part of the teaching job is for teachers to take part in teacher training and professional development programs. As shown in Pawan and Fan's Chapter 5, teachers are expected to meet in their teacher groups and attend district-level meetings and professional development sessions weekly, particularly to be updated on new ideas, policies, or testing requirements. Teacher training programs are also held in the summer or winter vacations. In the case of seasoned (senior) teachers and subject leader teachers (see Fan's Chapter 4), they spend time, in addition, helping new teachers by working jointly on lesson plans, observing classes, or opening their own classes for new teachers to learn from. The teachers are also often called upon to showcase demonstration classes to parents and "quality" inspectors who can include their principal and government officials. New teachers have to play their part in the same process but they, in addition, have to prepare and take part in regular high-stakes competition (see Pawan's Chapter 6). All teachers, however, have to undertake research and attempt to publish it to increase their promotional prospects.

As can be seen from the preceding paragraphs, despite the fewer hours of teaching when compared to teachers in the U.S., for example, Chinese teachers generally engage extensively with their students but this happens outside of classroom hours, more often than not until late in the day and into the evening, even spilling into the weekends as well. Teacher engagement in extra-curricular activities, however, is kept to a minimum; more often than not, these are reserved for practice sessions for special celebrations.

For Chinese teachers, their job is all-consuming and encompassing. Notwithstanding the situation, as can be seen from the teacher voices in the following section, there are multiple incentives for individuals to become a permanent teacher in the Chinese educational system.

The Bowl Offerings

In this section, transcripts from a group discussion between August and September 2016 yielded teachers' opinions and views regarding their profession. The participants in the discussions were twenty-one in-service teachers who maintain an online community with each other to share and exchange ideas regularly. They are graduates of normal schools, teacher colleges, and normal universities.

A grounded analysis of the transcript of the discussion yielded the following information as to the top-most reasons why these teachers plan to remain in the job for the long term (see Table 3.1).

TABLE 3.1 The Importance of a Permanent Teaching Job

Reasons	*Number of teachers*
1. Like the teaching profession	21
2. Stability	15
3. Favorable work environment	12
4. Benefits for children and family	10
5. Feeling of honor as a teacher	9
6. Winter and summer vacations	9
7. Salary	3

All the teachers unanimously agreed that they are teachers because they like the profession. There are two ways in which this sentiment was expressed, namely, in that they are in the job they have always aspired to be in and that they are rewarded by how it makes them feel about themselves. In terms of the former, the sentiment is elucidated by statements such as the following:

- As a child, I dreamed to be a teacher who can influence others.
- My English teacher in middle school was a role model to me and since then, I wanted to become a teacher.
- I grew up wanting to work with children.
- Teaching is a natural for me and fits my personality.

The following statements provide insight into how teaching is gratifying in various ways:

- I see progress every day in the classroom and I feel I am making a difference.
- I feel that I learn something new each day and improving myself.
- The job makes me feel that I am doing my part in being socially responsible.
- I enjoy standing in front of the classroom where I feel I make connections with my students.

The teachers are also in the job because of the stability it provides. The official ruling cited earlier indicates that in public schools, once teachers obtain permanent employment, it is rare that they lose their positions. In cases where there were teacher dismissals, they were those who violated Article 37 of the Teachers' Law of the People's Republic of China (Standing Committee of the National People's Congress, 1993) which states that teachers are dismissed on the following grounds:

- Deliberately and intentionally not accomplishing educational and teaching tasks;
- Continuing to administer corporal punishment on students despite admonishment;
- Behaving in improper and insulting ways toward students.

Even teachers who are ineffective and under-performing are often spared dismissal. Instead, they are usually reassigned to other schools or they are assigned to undertake service work that does not involve teaching.

The stability of the job comes with the "hukou", or an internal identification card or passport which entitles individuals to permanent residency in a location. One of the main criteria for individuals who apply for the hukou is permanent employment. In this regard teachers who secure such an employment in schools also secure permanent residency in the location where their schools are situated.

Job security and stability of residence, thus, go hand in hand as is evidenced by the following quote:

> Once you get a hukou, especially in big cities like Beijing, you belong to the place you work and you are secure with your job.
> *(Feng, senior high school teacher, August 26, 2016)*

The privileges also extend to family members and this is particularly the reason why many residents seek to attain the hukou, especially in what are known as first-tier cities, such as Beijing and Shanghai. With a hukou and a permanent job, teachers are allowed to enroll their own children in schools in the cities where they are employed and the benefits of such an advantage are significant:

> Local students in big cities have an incredible advantage in doing well in the gaokao (the university entrance examinations) because there are more resources. They also have opportunities to gain admission into key universities which are in those big cities as admission benchmarks are more favorable for students already in the cities.
> *(Lu, junior high school teacher, August 16, 2016)*

Stability in the job as a teacher thus has benefits that are wide-ranging and that include the welfare of a family. This is reiterated again in statements that speak to several of the highly ranked reasons behind why the permanent teaching job is greatly sought after:

- Teaching students also helps me to be a better teacher to my own children.
- With my own children in my school, I can keep track of them.
- Summer and winter vacations allow me to spend time with my family.
- Teaching allows me a schedule that is both predictable and flexible too. It is good for my children.

The regularity of the teaching schedule goes one step further to include spousal fidelity for one teacher:

> With not much time to spare during the week, our spouses do not worry that we will have love affairs outside our marriage.
> *(Shi, elementary school teacher, September 10, 2016)*

A favorable work environment was also cited as one of the reasons. Statements expressed indicate that the teachers feel that having a secure teaching job cocoons them in a workplace separated from the complexity of the outside world:

> In school, there is a pure environment. Relationships are well-defined. Work life is simple and straightforward. We do not need to go to many

social events where we could get into trouble because we say something we should not say.

(Mu, junior/middle school teacher, September 28, 2016)

There is also honor as a teacher in the workplace. Teachers have an important social position in the Chinese culture exemplified by statements such as the following:

- Teachers are the engineer of the human soul.
- Teachers are respected as people who impart knowledge and cultivate minds.
- People see me as a teacher, I help others. They acknowledge me.
- In people's mind, teachers have a high social value.

There is a special day honoring teachers on the tenth of September each year. Former students visit their teachers, who along with current students, bear gifts as ways to honor their teachers. Undeniably, however, in recent Chinese history, teachers were not so well considered, perceived as threats, and had their honorable status in society lowered. Nevertheless, throughout it all, in the minds of people in general, having teachers is as natural as having a parent and this is exemplified by the Chinese saying, "A teacher for a day is a father for life."

In their permanent position, teachers are assured an average salary between U.S. $17,000 to $18,000 in a country where the average income for middle-class families can range anywhere between U.S. $10,000 to $60,000 (Censky, 2012). It is considered a good salary to have, as according to one teacher ". . . the salary is less than the high and higher than the low" (Shin, high school teacher, September 16, 2016). Teachers could earn more if they teach in private schools. However, their chances for promotion there are non-existent (see Fan's Chapter 4). For this reason, as well as for the reason of avoiding unnecessary pressure from parents who are paying high fees, private schools are not the first choice for graduates except for those who are unable to qualify and find positions to teach in public schools.

All these reasons serve as significant incentives for teachers in the discussion group to stay in the job for the long term. At the macro level, the appeal of a permanent teaching job can also be further understood in the context where there is an increasing discourse to eliminate job security in a climate where unemployment and lack of job placement are seen as moving toward a crisis point in the country (Howard & Howard, 2007).

Cracks in the Bowl? Critical Thoughts and Conclusions

When the views in the preceding section are considered, a permanent public school teaching position is indeed an appealing and lucrative one. However, does the process to obtain it justify the professional end point? Let us take the certification examination process, for example. Although there are indeed positive positions about it, there are also the following views in the online discussion group that challenge its utility:

> A lot of time is spent preparing for the exam but its use is limited. Knowledge of the theories are easy to be forgotten right away after the exam.
>
> (Dong, middle school teacher, September 16, 2016)

> Some people worried that if the certificate test is so strict, nobody would want to take it. There will be fewer teachers at a time education is of great importance for our family, society and our nation. My belief is that instead of a test or exam, the government should raise teachers' salaries to attract more excellent people to join the profession!
>
> (Li, elementary school teacher, August 17, 2016)

These views converge with opinions of researchers such as Lin, Yu and Wu (2011) and Liu (2012) who worry that passing the examination will not guarantee teacher quality. The coverage, for example, of the examination, minimally, if at all, includes a focus on teaching ethics and the teaching of students with diverse ethnic backgrounds. Given the challenges that China is having with the issues of teacher character and the lack of teachers' knowledge and ability to work with a diverse population group (see Wang, Chapter 8), what is covered in the examination is insufficient and perfunctory. Passing the examination also may be out of reach for senior teachers who may not have the latest information and detrimental to those who may not have taken examinations for an extended length of time because it has been a long time since they left school.

Furthermore, there is also worry that provinces might skew the examination results so that they favor the performance of teachers in their own localities. Also, as with all examinations, what can be gained from them is limited, in terms of ensuring teacher quality. Just as Pawan mentioned in the introductory chapter, qualifications such as those based on terminal examinations only serve gate-keeping functions but they do not address professionalism. There is an often-quoted saying in China that describes the situation for teachers facing the examinations: "Examination only but education none" (只考不育, zhi kao bu yu).

The fact that a permanent teaching position is bound together with the hukou application process is problematic on several fronts. First and foremost, because the job as a permanent teacher for some is seen as a means to gain residency along with its related privileges, it may draw individuals who are not as committed to the profession and who see it merely as a stepping stone to other opportunities once residency is gained. Accordingly, it has led to the loss of talented teachers in the rural areas to big cities (see Wang's Chapter 8). Even without these considerations, the hukou system by itself has become a social issue. It is seen by some as a form of a "caste system" (Han, 1999) that places a barrier between urban and rural dwellers and the well-educated from those with fewer educational opportunities; and it contributes to "internal migrations" of epic proportions of workers to big cities, resulting in approximately 44 percent of the Chinese population now living in cities and straining their resources. Such large-scale migrations inevitably result in the breaking up of the nuclear family unit across the board.

In terms of teachers, in particular, because of the hukou privileges which allow them to enroll their children in their place of employment, it is not unusual to see teachers, especially female teachers, who along with their children, live in faraway cities or provinces from the spouses until their children graduate from high schools, a process that can take up almost twelve years or more. Such a situation is not ideal for marriages and may exacerbate a situation that is already worrying. Although nationally the divorce rate in China is between 2 to 3 percent, in big cities such as Beijing and Shanghai, the divorce rates are as high as 40 percent and it continues to rise (Florcruz, 2013).

Be that as it may, a permanent teaching job is still a highly sought after profession in China, particularly in the current climate. The political, economic, and demographic developments in the country are evolving and changing at a massive and an unprecedented scale. At the job front, changes at all these levels have led to an increase in the "informalization of employment" in which employment "is not stable or secure, that lacks a written agreement or contract, and that does not provide social insurance or benefits" (Gallagher et al., 2011, p. 2). They cite estimates that in big Chinese cities, up to 39 percent of employment is informal.

It is inconceivable at this point in time that permanent teaching jobs in public schools will go toward that direction in China as teaching as a profession is not taken lightly. Nevertheless, threats do exist including the status of the English language in the country and globally. (See Pawan and Yuan's Chapter 10.) The question is thus whether these threats and the current developments present new opportunities for teachers to approach their job differently.

References

Censky, A. (2012, June 26). China's middle class boom. *CNN Money*. Retrieved from http://money.cnn.com/2012/06/26/news/economy/china-middle-class/

Florcruz, M. (2013, February 27). China's divorce rates rises from seventh consecutive year. *International Business Times*. Retrieved from www.ibtimes.com/chinas-divorce-rate-rises-seventh-consecutive-year-1105053

Gallagher, M., Lee, C., Kuruvilla, S., Kuruvilla, S., Lee, C., & Gallagher, M. (2011). Introduction and argument. In *From iron rice bowl to informalization: Markets, workers, and the state in a changing China* (pp. 1–14). Cornell University Press. Retrieved from www.jstor.org/stable/10.7591/j.ctt7zbgc.3

Han, D. (1999). The Hukou system and China's rural development. *The Journal of Developing Areas*, *33*(3), 355–378. Retrieved from www.jstor.org/stable/4192870

Howard, P., & Howard, R. (2007). The campaign to eliminate job security in China. *Journal of Contemporary Asia, 25*(3), 338–355.

Lin, Q., Yu, Q., & Wu, J. Y. (2011). A reflection of the non-normal students' register of teacher certification test. *Education Exploration, 8,* 79–82.

Liu, X. J. (2012). Current situation, problems and solutions of preschool teacher certification system. *Journal of Tianjin Academy of Educational Sciences, 1,* 84–86.

Ministry of Education. (2001). *Guided principles on issues concerning the first time teacher certification.* Retrieved from www.moe.edu.cn/publicfiles/business/htmlfiles/moe/moe_16/201301/147248.html

Silbert, S. (2014, December 26). In China, civil service jobs lose some appeal amid graft crackdown. *Lost Angeles Times.* Retrieved from www.latimes.com/world/asia/la-fg-china-officials-20141226-story.html

Standing Committee of the National People's Congress. (1993). *Teachers' law of the People's Republic of China.* Retrieved from www.gov.cn/banshi/2005-05/25/content_937.htm

4

MASTER-NOVICE (SHIFU-TUDI) TEACHER RELATIONSHIPS

Acquiring Knowledge From the Backbone of Experience

Wenfang Fan

Introduction

New teachers lack teaching experience. In grade schools in China, besides acquiring teaching experience through teaching, they also learn knowledge about teaching from the experienced teachers. This learning of knowledge about teaching is done through a system based on a shifu-tudi (master-disciple) relationship. The term *shifu* (师傅) can be "used to refer to teachers who pass on expertise to others" (Grand Dictionary Editorial Board, 1979, pp. 60–61). *Tudi* (徒弟), on the other hand, "refers to people who follow the shifu to acquire certain expertise" (Grand Dictionary Editorial Board, 1979, p. 801). The "shitu" relationship, short for shifu-tudi, is the result of an apprenticeship system that has been described as one in which two people work together, with the more experienced helping and leading the way for the person who is new or less experienced. As is shown by the definitions of the two terms, shifu are considered superior to their tudi.

Shifu-tudi relationships exist in public schools, at the elementary, junior high (middle school), and senior high (high school) levels. The relationship is a form of a school-based professional development for young teachers.

The Background to the Shifu-Tudi Relationship

The shifu-tudi relationship has deep roots in Chinese society and is synonymous to a "father and son" relationship. When viewed from this perspective, what is true in the father-son relationship is also true for the shifu-tudi relationship in that:

- The shifu-tudi relationship is lifelong.
- A shifu has the responsibility to pass on knowledge or expertise to tudi.

- Like a father, shifu also have the power and responsibility to show care for and help tudi in daily life.
- Shifu are supposed to set a good example for tudi to follow in issues of ethics and morality.
- A single tudi can only have one shifu. (In extremely rare cases, the tudi might have another mentor only with the permission of the original shifu.)
- Tudi must always listen to their shifu like a son must always listen to his father. This means that the tudi must show comprehensive obedience to the shifu.

The relationship is typified in *Journey to the West* (Wu, 2007), one of the four most important and well-known classical Chinese mythological and historical novels. In the novel, the shifu, Monk Tang, led three of his followers on what was thought to be an impossible mission. The journey took them twenty years to complete after walking 108,000 miles, to obtain an original Buddhist scripture from India, a country known to the Chinese then as Western Heaven. Along the way they experienced eighty-one life-threatening circumstances. However, Monk Tan, as shifu, led his disciples (tudi) to success in overcoming all the obstacles because his tudi showed absolute obedience to his instructions to use their resources and talents. The first tudi, the monkey, had a golden staff as a weapon, could transform himself seventy-two times, and could fly; the second, a pig with a magic rake, had thirty-six transformations to his name and could walk on clouds; and the third had a moon fork as a weapon and a means to carry all their luggage and fight in water.

The presence of the shifu-tudi relationship in a classical and widely read novel signals its pervasiveness. It exists in professional fields such as in business in the relationship between executives and their subordinates; in the performance arts, between well-known and emerging performers; in specific trades such as in the relationship between skilled and unskilled craftsmen. The relationship between teachers and students is, nevertheless, the shifu and tudi relationship in the real sense if we go by the practices of Confucius (551 BC– 479 BC), the great Chinese philosopher and educator. (See also Pei, Pawan, and Jin's Chapter 1.) During his time, people in high social positions would hire learned scholars to teach their children in their homes. Other scholars ran private schools of their own attended by people from near and far who came to learn from them. In both situations, it was usually the case that one teacher had one student. However, when a shifu became popular, such as the case with Confucius, that arrangement quickly changed. In fact, Confucius as a shifu had 3,000 students and ran the largest and most famous private school during his time.

Confucius taught by using aphorisms in his lectures as a means to teach his disciples various types of knowledge for the purposes of improving their character and conduct. Paintings show him sitting on the floor in front of students lecturing on a wide range of social and political topics as well as on literature and art forms (e.g., poetry, calligraphy, music). Ethics and morality were the central themes across the topics which he also exemplified through his behavior and practices. What Confucius said and did were written down by his followers. After he died, the writings resulted in a collection of Confucius's teachings and his conversations with his students named *The Analects of Confucius*.

Official Positions on Shifu-Tudi Relationships

In official governmental documents pertaining to school practices, the term *shifu-tudi* is not used outright but it is the basis of working relationships that are expected between experienced and new teachers. This is evident in the documents *Trial Regulations on the Professional Positions of Public School Teachers* (National Education Committee, 1986) and *Regulations on Selecting Special Class Teacher* (National Teaching Committee, 1993). Both documents stress that senior, experienced, and well-known teachers are to be in charge of training new teachers in all aspects including in the preparation of teaching, classroom instruction, correcting students' homework, and giving students tests. The more experienced teachers are also to be responsible and resourceful in raising young teachers' morality, knowledge, and teaching ability.

There is also an official document that specifies the extent and ways that shifu (experienced teachers) should train tudi (new teachers). According to the document *Proposals on Carrying out Training of New Teachers in Elementary Schools During the Trial Period* (State Education Commission, 1994), two-thirds of the training of new teachers should be their tutelage in school under the guidance of their shifu. The guidance must be undertaken daily and within the one-year trial period for new teachers, in no less than 120 class periods (4 class periods each week); new teachers must also spend time in concentrated training where experienced teachers arrange specific times, locations, and topics to cover in great detail. The time spent and allocated for the shifu-tudi training in schools is closely and seriously monitored by officials from the local government.

Shifu-Tudi Relationships in Classroom Practice

Although the official documents and directives exist, each school has the freedom to find ways to put into place the shifu-tudi system that works best in its context. The research of Lv (1963) and Zhang and Zhang (1985) are insightful as they help to provide a framework for the practice in general. In one of the first articles about the subject of shifu-tudi, entitled *How We Train Our Young Teachers*, Lv (1963) described how the first group of graduates from a high school in 1953 were retained as teachers in the same school. Although, since then, teachers are also hired from elsewhere, the way they were trained in the shifu-tudi system

TABLE 4.1 Shifu-Tudi Mentoring Practices

Guidance by experienced teachers	Methods of training young teachers
Experienced teachers showcase and reflect on own classroom teaching	After young teachers observed the experienced teachers' class, the latter in detail, reflect and identify the strong points and weak points of their own teaching.
Experienced teachers observe young teachers classroom teaching	After observing young teachers' class, experienced teachers comment on the teaching that took place.
Experienced teachers organize peer-to-peer observations	Young teachers observe and comment on each other's teaching and consult their experienced teachers.
Experienced teachers organize and undertake theme-based lectures	After obtaining information from the various observations, experienced teachers provide young teachers with lectures on the topics that are most relevant.
Impromptu and "any time" discussion	Experienced teachers provide timely and casual feedback and invite young teachers to initiate discussions about teaching at any point in time.

in Lv's research still rings true to the present day. In Lv's description, experienced teachers helped young teachers with lesson preparation by selecting textbook content and showing ways to teach them, modeling instruction by opening their own classrooms for observations, and providing feedback and comments on classes taught by the new teachers. To Lv, this was the most efficient way of training new teachers.

In an article in *People's Daily*, twenty-two years later, Zhang and Zhang (1985) provided a similar but more refined description of the shifu mentoring practices of a Special Grade Teacher named Yu Yi. Yu's description has become a fundamental guide as to how shifu-tudi relationships could be undertaken, as described in Table 4.1.

The Identification of Shifu: The Unveiling of a School Hierarchy

Theoretically speaking, any teacher with more than three years of teaching experience can be a shifu to a new teacher, but in practice, shifu is often chosen from experienced teachers with prestigious professional titles which are attained through accumulated achievements and credentials.

The school-level titles are based on grade levels that teachers teach. In primary schools, professional titles are in the ascending order of Elementary Two, Elementary One, Elementary High, and Middle High. In middle and high schools, the titles to be attained are Middle Two, Middle One, and High School. The professional titles are given to teachers based on many factors including years of teaching and excellence in undertaking research about teaching and in public service. Technically, all of the titles can be achieved within three years except for the High School title which takes at least five years and thus is the most difficult to achieve. These professional titles are predetermined and permanent, which means that once middle school teachers, for example, are promoted to high, they will always have the title. For all teachers, their first objective is to be promoted as teachers with these school-level titles.

There is another line of professional advancement that entitles teachers to be a shifu and this is through public recognition of them as leading figures in their professional field, which in the case of this book, is English language teaching. There are three titles to be attained this way and they are the titles of the Backbone Teacher (骨干教师, gugan jiaoshi), the Subject Leading Figure (学科带头人, xueke daitouren), and Special Class Teacher (特级教师, teji jiaoshi). The recognition of teachers as Backbone Teacher or Subject Leading Figure is undertaken at the district level and the city level, respectively, with the latter having a higher level of visibility. To be recognized as either one, teachers need credentials that attest to their teaching abilities and experience. For example, they can achieve the credentials by undertaking public demonstration classes at the highest grade levels, winning multiple teaching competitions (see Pawan's Chapter 6), undertaking impactful research that is published, mentoring extensively and having apprentices who have themselves won awards. Each school gets allocations from the district administration as to how many Subject Leading Figures and Backbone Teachers they can select per term. To make this system dynamic, the titles are held at three-year terms. At the end of three years, teachers need to apply again for the recognition. Being recognized as a Subject Leading Figure or a Backbone Teacher is a great honor and the recognition means chances and opportunities, for example, to give demonstration classes on major occasions such as on Teacher Day celebrations and to be recommended to participate in competitions representing the district or the city.

At present, teachers with both titles also receive monetary awards in addition to their salary. The amount of money given to them varies from place to place and the affordability levels of their schools and districts at a particular time. At present, a Backbone Teacher, in a major city, could receive about 500 yuan and a Subject Leading Figure, 600 yuan a month (U.S. $75–100), amounts which are roughly twenty times higher than the financial awards in the previous decade. The teachers often say that the money, although not much, is an incentive. What counts the most, however, is the honor that comes with the titles.

The highest title to be achieved for advancement is the Special Class Teacher title, a lifelong title. It is a recognition that applies across provinces as well as at the national level and given only to a limited number of individuals. In a province, there might only be one or two teachers recognized every five years and there are times when not even one teacher is recognized at all with that title within that time period. Although there maybe provincial variations of specific expectations, there are overall requirements for teachers to qualify as a Special Class Teacher. In particular, teachers must have an established track record of excellence in teaching and in examination performance. In terms of the former, it is expected that they have successfully acquired teaching honors at multiple levels (e.g., at the governmental, national, local districts), that are obtained through various means, including most important, through competitions whereby they have to have won first prize and first place at each of those levels. Research publications also take up a large percentage of the consideration for the title and in some cases teachers must have published three papers in provincial- or national-level journals and have won first- or second-place prizes in journal article competitions at the provincial levels or higher. Furthermore, teachers must be able to provide proof of undertaking public service which goes above and beyond what is required for Subject Leading Figures and Backbone Teachers. Finally, Special Class Teacher hopefuls must also demonstrate a strong command and knowledge of their subject area through an examination which can count toward 50 percent of how they are assessed. In the examination, teachers are tested not only on their English proficiency but also on current teaching methods and educational theories. Like all examinations, the Special Class Teacher examinations are closely guarded secrets and confidential.

In a word, the process for teachers to apply for the Special Class title is rigorous and thus, most teachers do not attempt it. However, for those who do and are successful, they are much admired and highly sought after as a shifu. This award and the others previously described demonstrate the hierarchical system that exists in Chinese schools and amongst teachers. Navigating through the system is the task that tudi undertake in relationships with their shifu.

The Taxonomy of Shifu-Tudi Relationships

There are two ways in which this shifu-tudi relationship is established: formal and informal. Each will be described in this section with material gained from interviews with five teachers (see Table 4.2).

TABLE 4.2 Shifu-Tudi Interviewees

Names (Pseudonyms)	Years of teaching	School levels
Teacher Nuo	28 years	elementary school
Teacher Ji	43 years	elementary school
Teacher Min	25 years	elementary school
Teacher Lei	3 years	senior high school
Administrator Shen	13 years	junior high school/middle school

They all have served as shifu as well as tudi and were able to shed light on the relationship.

Formal Shifu-Tudi Relationships

Although the relationship is a common practice in schools, it is often undertaken formally, even appearing as a requirement in schools' handbooks for new teachers. The formal process begins with the teachers being assigned to a shifu at the point when they register on the first day of their new job. In some schools, there is a ceremony in which the shifu and tudi will have a photograph taken together that is put on a certificate or letter of appointment, cementing the relationship between the two. The shifu and tudi usually teach the same subject at the same grade level, although sometimes that comes about in a roundabout way:

> My shifu majored in Japanese instead of English. She was assigned to be a teacher of English when there was a lack of English teachers. Like the other English teachers then, she taught English in Chinese. She is my shifu now because she is teaching English and at the same level like me.
> *(Teacher Nuo, elementary school, November 18, 2015)*

As new teachers progress, they may be assigned to new grades to teach but at the elementary schools, their shifu will remain the same. At the middle and high school levels, however, they may be assigned to new shifu who teach at the same grade that they do. Nevertheless, the change in shifu rarely happens except when a shifu moves to another school or when there are unresolvable conflicts between shifu and tudi.

The mentoring relationship in this formal arrangement follow written requirements set by each school. Besides modeling instruction, attending tudi's classes, helping with teaching preparations, and classroom management mentioned earlier, shifu help tudi with research into teaching, which new teachers in some schools must report to have accomplished at the end of each year. Most important, as described in Pawan's Chapter 6, shifu need to spend a lot of time and energy helping young teachers structure and practice for public teaching demonstrations or competitions. To achieve all these goals, schools specify the number of hours shifu and tudi need to attend each other's classes, anywhere from 20–40 classes (45 minutes per class) every semester and this arrangement can last up to three years for some teachers. Both shifu and tudi are given a special notebook to keep track of how they met the shifu-tudi requirements. In the notebooks, they also have to write down the thrust of the discussions they had together, including shifu's comments on tudi's reflections of their teaching.

It is clear from the formality and the amount of work required that the shifu-tudi arrangement in the schools is considered an important and highly valued school-based professional development.

Personal and Informal Mentoring Relationships

Teachers can also informally identify their own "shifu" to work with. There are no official agreements or documents to sign. Individuals may approach on their own a more experienced colleague for mentoring. Furthermore, teachers may approach other teachers who have natural leadership skills and experience even though they have not been recognized or have won awards. In this way, the shifu-tudi relationship is undertaken voluntarily and informally. For Teacher Ji, to be chosen in such a way can be gratifying:

> I have my own tudi in my school. But many other young teachers ask me to be their shifu, too. I don't even know why. It always makes me feel great.
> *(Teacher Ji, elementary school, November 18, 2015)*

In this relationship, the tudi would attend shifu's classes more often than the reverse and make their own arrangements to meet the shifu. The onus is on the tudi to make the relationship work, the success of which depends on how dedicated and eager the tudi are in teaching and in enlisting their shifu's assistance:

> It all depends on the young teachers. If they, the tudi, show great passion and make huge efforts to improve and grow professionally, shifu would do a lot to help. The young teachers become good teachers faster. As a result, both shifu and tudi are satisfied with each other and feel honored.
> *(Teacher Min, elementary school, November 23, 2015)*

There is no official recognition of the work done by the shifu and tudi when the relationship is developed informally in this way. However, and because this is the case, there is often a strong sense of gratitude on the part of the tudi because of the help the shifu provided without being required to do so:

> You know my shifu is 65 years old now. She retired from her job a few years ago. I often go to see her. I am so grateful to her because of her help and advice when she was my shifu in school. She is like my mother.
> *(Teacher Nuo, elementary school, November 18, 2015)*

The Prospects of Continuation

When asked about the shifu-tudi system, one teacher proclaimed the following:

> . . . the shifu-tudi relationship will always be there. In China, you have to follow the Chinese tradition.
> *(Teacher Min, elementary school, November 23, 2015)*

This quote suggests that the continuation of this system and the relationship that emerges are a cultural staple. For new teachers, they are a practical necessity as having a shifu equals having someone to rely on for support to ease their transition into teaching, during a very vulnerable time at the beginning of their tenure as teachers:

> It gives a great feeling to know that you can have someone you can go to when you have questions. I didn't even know how to start when I first came to the school. But I was not too afraid. The "shitu" relationship makes me feel I am not alone in doing everything. I'm very grateful to my shifu.
> *(Teacher Lei, senior high, June 12, 2015)*

Research findings from Zhang's (2009) study echo the previous quote. Zhang (2009) demonstrated that the essential nature of the shifu-tudi system centers on the emotional support it provides young teachers. In particular, it alleviates the transition shock into the world of employment which unless dealt with immediately and compassionately can lead to early burnout for young teachers. Hence, the shifu provide new teachers with empathetic and sustained support that can be resorted to when needed.

The shifu-tudi system will also prevail because shifu can provide advice that is grounded in the reality of the tudi because both are together on a daily basis. And because they teach alongside their tudi, shifu can provide "just-in-time" assistance. The two quotes below are illustrative:

> My shifu attends my class. She praises me but also tells me about problems while I am teaching. For example, she said I spoke too fast in class. I didn't give time and chances for students to talk. I could fix the problems immediately.
> *(Teacher Lei, senior high, June 12, 2015)*

> What I mostly learned from my shifu was how she interpreted the texts in the textbooks. After I observed her classes, I knew how to locate the key points in a text to teach and knew my goal of teaching of a lesson each day.
> *(Teacher Nuo, elementary school, November 18, 2015)*

The quotes reiterate Shen, Chen and Yu's (1995) assertion that the shifu-tudi mentoring relationship is most useful in the improvement of novice teachers' pedagogy, even more so than their improvement of subject matter knowledge. This is particularly the case when mentoring practices are put into place systematically and comprehensively. Fan and Liao's study (2012) demonstrates how these could be achieved through three stages of shifu-tudi mentoring. First is the adaption stage where shifu help novice teachers to orient themselves to their teaching roles and environment; second, the development stage where the teachers are guided in ways to improve their teaching and classroom management abilities as well as to establish new achievement goals; and finally, third, is the individual growth stage where the teachers are guided to reflect on their own teaching styles and then to assume autonomy to develop creatively and innovatively.

The shifu-tudi mentoring relationship will continue as it will pay off in the long run as well. For the tudi, the relationship can open doors to opportunities and networks of individuals that the new teachers may find difficult to access otherwise:

> Besides helping me with teaching and with research, my shifu introduces me to the district and provincial level administrators. By knowing them I might get chances to give demo lessons and can take part in important teaching contests.
> *(Teacher Min, elementary school, November 23, 2015)*

For the shifu, the responsibility to be a mentor improves their prospects of promotion to the higher levels of the profession. This is because the success of their tudi is also viewed as the success of their shifu, which is a pre-requisite, as mentioned earlier, for the latter to qualify for promotion and elevated titles.

In addition to these teacher-based reasons, the shifu-tudi system of training and professional development will be sustained because it is also a money- and time-saving way for schools. Because they are using in-house staff members and school time to train teachers, schools do not have to spend additional funds, which they would have to do if they only rely on external experts to be brought in or if their teachers have to leave their classrooms for extra training.

Continued existence of the shifu-tudi system in public schools is also assured because pedagogical training and professional development in comprehensive and normal universities and normal schools is insufficient. As described in Pei, Pawan, and Jin's Chapter 1, pedagogical courses are minimal in comparison to subject matter courses which can be as low as one-fifth of the overall coursework offered at the tertiary levels. Also, as was shown in Pei and Jin's Chapters 2, there is a limited period of time and few opportunities for pre-service teachers to practice teaching and to develop pedagogical expertise.

Hence, the prospect for the continuation of the shifu-tudi system in public schools is bright as it is necessary and will probably be in place for the long term. Nevertheless, there are challenges to the system that could alter the very nature of its current form.

Challenges and Changes to a Revered System

Every coin has two sides and so is the case with the shifu-tudi system. Along with its strengths, the system has its shortcomings as well. First, the one-to-one shifu-tudi relationship can be limiting as we will see in the jiaoyanzu chapter

(Pawan and Fan's Chapter 5). Wang (1999) pointed out that the quality of shifu largely decides the outcome of the mentoring. Because of the Chinese hierarchical tradition, it is the shifu who dominate and have the upper hand in such a relationship. Shifu who are rigid in their ways could restrict their tudi's exercise of autonomy and creativity in teaching (Shen et al., 1995).

Furthermore, the face-saving and promotional elements of the shifu-tudi relationship are also worrisome as tudi's achievements can reflect on the public face and the promotional prospects of their shifu. Such a situation can create unnecessary pressure on both the tudi and the shifu. The latter, if they are self-absorbed and irresponsible, may see the teaching job as a pursuit of one title after another and may exert unnecessary pressure on new teachers whom they see as instruments of their success.

The shifu-tudi system can also be a way for school administrators to undertake a form of surreptitious quality control. They can use the system as a means to keep both experienced teachers and new teachers accountable and "on their toes" on the job. The system can be perceived as a stifling "big-brother" system where everyone feels that they are constantly being monitored. This is implied in the following statement from the chair of a department who was praising the shifu-tudi system:

> Having a responsibility to be a shifu is a reminder for experienced teachers to behave themselves and to work well because that they are being followed and observed by their tudi.
> *(Administrator Shen, junior and senior high, March 8, 2016)*

The foregoing reasons may be the impetus for the changes being considered to the shifu-tudi system. To offset the intensity of the one-to-one relationship, for example, Shen et al. (1995) and Zhou (2004) proposed a more communal form of shifu-tudi system as an alternative. Shifu should consist of a collection or group of experienced teachers that all tudi could go to. Tudi should also form their own community of practice in which they tutor and support each other. In such a way, tudi are not bound to a single individual for advice but instead will benefit from the perspectives of multiple shifu. In their own peer-group, tudi teachers could benefit from the freedom of being able to engage with other individuals who have access to and are comfortable with resources and ways of thinking that reflect their generation, education, and exposure.

Changes at the macro level can also alter organically the nature of the shifu-tudi relationship and configuration. For one, technology has the potential in China to decentralize and democratize everyone's access to information (Ran & Qi, 2005). In this regard, young teachers who are tudi will be not be restricted to human mentors for information which can now be multi-sourced and multi-modal in nature. Having such a facility challenges the pedestal that shifu have placed themselves on as their tudi do not have to rely solely on them for the latest and for the most innovative information in order to be responsive in the classroom. Unfortunately, Chinese university teacher training and professional development programs have yet to fully realize this potential (Chen, 2003; Xiao, 2007).

China's undeniable prosperity has also shifted the knowledge playing field, particularly where English is concerned. Many tudi of the current generation may be better informed and more proficient in the language than their shifu are. (See also Pawan's Chapter 6.) This is because a large number of Chinese people have been able to travel overseas to English-speaking countries; for example, the number reached 3,050,000 people in 2013 (Pan, 2014). People are also able to send their children overseas for schooling and to increase their exposure to the language. For example, in 2012, Chinese overseas high school students accounted for 22.6 percent of the total number of such students in the U.S. (Liu, 2012). Parents can also now afford to hire native English language speaker tutors for them at home (De, 2012; Liu, 2012; Pan, 2014). In such cases, especially for students in well-resourced schools from wealthy homes, the students may outshine their teachers in terms of English language proficiency. Accordingly, new teachers emerging from this generation may have English language skills that exceed those of their shifu/mentors and thus may consider them and their advice obsolete. However, whether or not the challenge to the shifu status in this way is imminent is questionable as inequity in educational opportunities and wealth disparities continue to exist in China. In other words, not everyone will feel the immediate benefit of Chinese prosperity in ways that could equally uplift them all educationally. And in that regard, it is even further away from being a threat to the shifu-tudi tradition in the Chinese educational system.

References

Chen, G. M. (2003). The reasons and countermeasures of low using rate of multimedia devices in rural middle schools. *Guizhou Education, 2*, 42–43.

De, Y. (2012). The number of Chinese young overseas students increases more than 100 times in 5 years accompanied by many psychological problems. *Overseas Chinese, 4*, 61–62.

Fan, W., & Liao, Q. (2012). The connotations and features based on shifu-tudi relationship in teachers' professional development. *Journal of Educational Development, 9*(1), 45–47.

Grand Dictionary Editorial Board. (1979). *The Grand Dictionary*. Shanghai: Shanghai Dictionary Publishing House.

Liu, X. Y. (2012). Chinese high school overseas student accounting for 22.6% of total overseas students. *Children's Study, 3*, 59.

Lv, Q. H. (1963). How we train our young teachers. *People's Education, 12*, 52–53.

National Education Committee. (1986). *Trial regulations on the professional positions of public school teachers*. Ministry of Education of People's Republic of China. Retrieved from www.moe.edu.cn/publicfiles/business/htmlfiles/moe/s7077/201412/180698.html

National Teaching Committee. (1993). *Regulations on selecting special class teacher*. Ministry of Education of People's Republic of China. Retrieved from www.moe.edu.cn/publicfiles/business/htmlfiles/moe/moe_621/201001/81916.html

Pan, Y. (2014). Chinese overseas students in 2013. *World Education Information, 5*, 78.

Ran, X. Y., & Qi, X. L. (2005). Use the advantages of modern distance education to enhance balanced development of education. *Education Exploration, 1*, 56–57.

Shen, L., Chen, X. Y., & Yu, Y. (1995). The teacher training model of "Shi-Tu-Help-Lead": A comparative study of the Chinese and American young teachers training at their beginning teaching professional career. *Foreign Education Material, 1995*(5), 56–62.

State Education Commission. (1994). *Proposals on carrying out training of new teachers in elementary schools during the trial period*. Hubei Provincial Department of Education. Retrieved from www.hbe.gov.cn/content.php?id=1095

Wang, X. M. (1999). A study of the difficulties encountered by new teachers: On drawbacks of the traditional education in the normal university. *Shanghai Research on Education, 4*, 34–36.

Wu, C. E. (2007). *Journey to the West*. Beijing: People's Literature Publishing House.

Xiao, Y. (2007). An analysis and countermeasures of multimedia devices lay unused in public schools. *Data of Culture and Education, 5*, 113–114.

Zhang, Q. (2009). *A case study on Apprenticeship and new teacher's professional development*. (Unpublished master dissertation). East China Normal University, Shanghai.

Zhang, Y. F., & Zhang, X. S. (1985). Famous special class teacher Yu Yi talks about "experienced teachers help newcomers." *People's Daily, 9*, 11.

Zhou, W. H. (2004). *Mentor model of new teachers in middle school: Taking Changshu city as an example*. (Unpublished master dissertation). East China Normal University, Shanghai.

5
SCHOOL-BASED PROFESSIONAL DEVELOPMENT WITH "JIAOYANZU" PEERS

Learning With Brothers and Sisters[1]

Faridah Pawan and Wenfang Fan

Introduction

The current research is an exploratory investigation of teacher professional development during the 2011–2012 academic year. We were involved in the professional development of Chinese English language teachers (ELTs) in three schools (elementary, middle, and high schools) in Beijing's northwest area. In the schools, teachers worked intensively with peers in "jiaoyanzu" or teacher research groups. We found ourselves pursuing a question that emerged from our joint experiences there, namely, the type of knowledge that emerges when teachers reflected with peers. We were interested in teacher reflections for their contributions to the professional development of the Chinese ELTs with whom we were working in particular and with language teachers in general.

Research Setting

In the schools we were attached to, much of the in-service teacher professional development (PD) was school-based and involved working in "jiaoyanzu" groups under the guidance of senior and experienced teachers. (Although jiaoyanzu is literally translated from Mandarin as "teacher research groups," they are defined primarily by peer mentoring activities in all aspects of teaching.) Each group consists of six to eight teachers, including a head teacher assigned by the principal. Usually a "backbone" or model teacher (mófàn jiàoshī) is also in the group, that is, someone most experienced in the subject area, and who might also be the head teacher. New teachers are also assigned mentors from the jiaoyanzu who provide individual support.

The teachers we worked with share a spacious office space reserved for English teachers. In that space, they spend a great deal of time in proximity with each other because most teach only two or three 40-minute periods a day or ten to twelve periods a week, especially at the middle and high school levels. (American middle and high school teachers generally teach 15–20 periods a week.) In these offices, ideas are shared, plans are revised, and resources are prioritized, of which the most important are teaching PowerPoints that are central in public school teaching. Additionally, new and veteran teachers develop PowerPoints for each other as they share mandated teaching texts and follow prescribed curricula outlined by the approved textbooks. Discussions often center on how to use the PowerPoints to teach the textbooks.

Teachers also meet weekly to discuss all aspects of teaching and school-related affairs including test preparation, schedules, teaching research projects, and government regulations. A very important feature of these meetings is the preparation of new and younger teachers (less than forty years old) for demonstration teaching (open classes) or teaching competitions, which happen at least twice a year. These teachers undertake frequent observations to learn from each other and from experts. The teachers are also frequently observed (we saw over fifteen observations in one semester) by head, backbone, and mentor teachers and peers who belong to the jiaoyanzu. (In addition, each classroom is also videotaped and channeled live to the principal's office.) The visits and briefings that follow are a means not only to evaluate but also to support teachers through feedback and suggestions for improvement. Thus, additionally, during these meetings, senior members of the jiaoyanzu group often report best practices they observed when attending national teaching competitions in other provinces. Thus, teachers extensively reflect through intensive study, practice, discussions, and observations, all aspects of their teaching with each other.

In addition to the school-based meetings, jiaoyanzu teachers are also expected to attend district-level weekly or biweekly meetings to be updated on all aspects of teaching, including best practices, test preparation, and upcoming initiatives at the district, provincial, and governmental levels. Finally, as part of the jiaoyanzu, the teachers have to take part in research projects as a means of teacher learning. Each project's focus is determined by the principal or leader of the research group. The teachers submit research findings and report on their publications and other accomplishments in an annual merit report.

Thus, jiaoyanzu activities consist of collective and reflective processes in which members peer-coach each other and are frequently present in each other's classrooms. Senior and model teachers are expected to "bring along the young" (lao dai qing) (Paine, 1990), namely, to mentor and support younger teachers in all ways. Not surprisingly, jiaoyanzu teachers often describe themselves as "sisters and brothers in a family" to express the tight interconnectedness of their working lives.

Literature Review

Reflective Teaching Research

Reflective teaching has become the focus of efforts to bridge the gap between teaching theory and practice. Recognition of reflective teaching is the recognition of the value of teacher insider knowledge (Bailey, Curtis & Nunan, 1998; Korthagen, 2001) to build the linkage between what has long separated researchers from practitioners. In this perspective, teachers are not viewed as the empty vessel or passive recipient of knowledge but are recognized as those who contribute to the construction of teaching knowledge based on what they know about themselves as learners, the sociocultural contexts in which they work, and the teaching and learning processes that take place in their classrooms (Freeman & Johnson, 1998). Reflection is also considered an essential component of teachers' growth and professionalism. Kyriacou (1994), for example, asserts that teachers are "the main agents of change of their own professional growth . . . in that teachers who regularly think of their own teaching are more likely to develop and improve their classroom practice" (p. 10). Intentional reflection also informs teachers of who they are and what their expertise is and thus, in this way professionalizes them (Peck & Westgate, 1994).

Interest in reflective practices has resulted in numerous research undertakings to understand what it constitutes. These undertakings provide a foundation for how reflective teaching is conceived. Rogers (2001) reviews the conceptual bases of reflection and their implication to teaching practice through the work of individuals including Dewey, Loughran, Mezirow, Seibert and Daudelin, Langer, Boud, Keogh and Walker, and Schön (p. 37). The contributions of the different individuals are analyzed along seven lines of inquiry including that of reflection's terminology, definitions, antecedents, context, process, outcomes, and techniques. For instance, with regard to terminology, Rogers identifies three categories covering no fewer than fifteen terms, namely (1) general terms (e.g., Dewey's (1933) reflective thought); (2) terms based on the timing of reflection (e.g., Schön's (1983) reflection-in-action); and (3) terms on the content of reflection (e.g., Mezirow's (1991) transformative learning model consisting of content, process, and premise reflection). The terminology studies suggest a need for a conceptualization consensus in order to achieve the "widest understanding and application of reflection" (p. 49).

Another example of a research line in reflective teaching is in the process of reflection in which there is agreement that effective reflection begins with the process of problem identification. Langer (1997), for instance, focuses on individuals' mindfulness as a means to engage individuals' active reflection; and Loughran (1996) incorporates suggestion and intellectualization of the problem once it is identified. In the process studies, researchers are cautioned not to formularize or oversimplify reflection. What is important is the nurturing of teachers' capability to make a conscious choice to reflect and to be intentional about the purposes of their reflection (Rogers, 2001, p. 52). Overall, Rogers's review highlights that reflection enhances teachers' learning and their "personal and professional effectiveness" (p. 49).

Marcos and Tillema (2006) in their review take a more direct approach by asking the question of the contributions of reflection studies on actual teaching. They identify two issues in the studies that impact the studies' relevancy, namely: the problem of the fragmentation of reflective studies that enable them to "tell only half the story"; and the problem of reporting outcomes that are more than can be known (p. 114). To help them gauge how closely the research studies address the two problems and, in essence, are effective in linking reflection to the process of teaching, Marcos and Tillema develop an analytical framework consisting of four criteria viz., "talking the talk," "talking the walk," "walking the talk," and "walking the walk" (p. 115).

The criterion, "talking the talk," focuses on descriptive studies on teachers' voices that explain how they interpret their practice. For example, Smith's (2005) study focused on experienced and novice teacher beliefs on characteristics of a good teacher. In "talking the walk," Marcos and Tillema review research that dealt with reported action. Meijer, Zanting, and Verloop (2002), for example, used videotaped lessons and stimulated recall interviews with twenty experienced teachers to engage them in describing the thinking behind their teaching as they watched the lessons. "Walking the talk" is represented by studies that outline the relationship between an intention and the action sequence that follows. This type of reflection is identified as the process of prospective reflection (Van Manen cited in Marcos & Tillema, 2006). An example study is that of Conway's (2001) in which teacher interns graphically depicted, wrote, and talked about what they anticipated and later what they remembered from their teaching experiences. The study allowed for the capturing of prospective reflections and the evaluation and comparison of actual teaching performances. Finally, "walking the walk" covers studies whereby teachers' actions are observed to see whether they exemplify teachers' knowledge. John (2002) observed the teaching of two teacher educators and interviewed them on their experiences, assumptions, and expertise afterward in their workplaces. His content analysis of time-ordered narratives and field notes led to the introduction of four dimensions of the educators' practical knowledge of teaching, namely, intentionality, practicality, subject specificity, and ethicality. Marcos and Tillema, at the end of the day, describe how difficult it is for studies to bridge the worlds of talk and walk, namely, to bridge reflection and practice/action. As a proposed solution, they introduce standards in the aforementioned four criteria to assess studies that attempt to make the bridge, namely, in talking the talk, the standard of non-framing and openness should apply; in talking the walk, authenticity; walking the talk, intentionality; finally, in walking the walk, the standard of situatedness, whereby findings are contextualized within the specificities of circumstances.

The coverage of reflective studies is far and wide as has been shown. Future trends can be observed in research in the area that have begun to emerge. Most significant of them all, given the post-modernity and criticality frameworks in the current academic discourse, is an exploration of critical reflection. Howard (2003), for example, looked at critical reflection in teaching, and in particular, as a foundation for the inclusion of culturally relevant pedagogy in ethnically diverse classrooms. Fook, White, and Gardner (2006, p. 13) define critical reflection as "reflective abilities to achieve some freeing from hegemonic assumptions." Citing Brookfield, Fook et al. (2006, p. 8) point out that "reflection is important for the daily business of living, but that critical reflection . . . is vital if we are to make crucially relevant changes. . . ."

The present research extends the discussion as it pertains to the knowledge that emerges from the reflections that might be useful for teachers' professional development. We describe the different types of knowledge emerging when the teachers reflected with their jiaoyanzu peers and then we compare them with knowledge that emerges when the teachers reflected on their own.

Sociocultural Perspective on Teacher Knowledge Base and Professional Development

The jiaoyanzu's prevalent role in Chinese ELTs' lives is especially noteworthy in light of the teachers' lengthy and rigorous pre-service training programs (three to four years; 96–128 credit hours), covering both content and pedagogy particularly if they attended normal (teaching) universities. The teachers also have to study for and complete rigorous teacher certification examinations. In addition, the ELTs undergo at least three hours per week of formal professional development offered by district and provincial governments. The prevalence of the jiaoyanzu thus represents recognition that teacher knowledge base development and learning are best achieved through engagement among teachers with experiences in a shared context.

Vygotsky (1978) argued that knowledge is mediated through social and cultural artifacts. He stressed that people learn through participating in social activities and they develop their cognition and unique ways of thinking through the interaction with the social and cultural contexts. This sociocultural perspective proposes that human thinking and behaviors cannot be analyzed and understood by looking at the individual in isolation, but rather embedded in social engagements in the contexts of politics, culture, and history. Johnson (2006) describes this epistemological shift that impacts teacher learning, as evolving "from behaviorist, to cognitive, to situated, social and distributed views of human cognition" (p. 236). She wrote:

> The epistemological stance of the sociocultural turn defines human learning as a dynamic social activity that is situated in physical and social contexts, and distributed across persons, tools, and activities.
>
> (p. 237)

The sociocultural perspective has thus validated the conception of teachers as "socioprofessionals" (Freeman, 2009, p. 15), whose knowledge and learning are embedded in their participation in social practices. As Freeman argues, disciplinary knowledge (applied linguistics, second language acquisition, literature and culture) accompanied with pedagogical knowledge of how to teach falls short of developing the professional unless the two are situated within the interpersonal interactions and activities within the contexts in which the teaching takes place. In this regard Freeman (2009) expands the gyre of the professional development of language teachers to encompass what he calls *substance, engagement* and *outcomes* (p. 15). The expansion focuses on social and intellectual scaffolds for teachers that "build toward fully competent professional participation" (p. 17). Freeman is pushing for the movement away from ad hoc or casual teacher engagement with each other (e.g., group study) to a deliberate use of participation and social engagement for learning.

The central constructs of sociocultural theory provide us with deeper insights into the juxtaposition of content, process, and sociocultural participation in teacher knowledge base and development. Johnson and Golombek (2003) argue that sociocultural theory is a useful theoretical framework to explain the processes of teacher learning in terms of the three key components: (a) internalization and transformation; (b) the zone of proximal development (ZPD); and (c) mediational means. In terms of the first component, namely, internalization and transformation, sociocultural theory focuses on how an individual moves back and forth from external activities to internal and cognitive analyses. In this process, the internal and external transform each other. The authors state that, "Internalization involves a process in which a person's activity is initially mediated by other people or cultural artifacts but later comes to be controlled by the person as he or she appropriates resources to regulate his or her own activities" (p. 731). The second component points to social mediation occurring in what Vygotsky defined as the zone of proximal development (ZPD), which suggests that people can advance in knowledge through collaboration with other, more capable individuals and resources. Finally, the third component delineates that within the ZPD, mediational means include three levels (Johnson & Golombek, 2003): other-regulation (e.g., talking with other teachers), object-regulation (e.g., lesson plan), and self-regulation (e.g., keeping personal teaching diaries). This mediation allows teachers to experience a transformative and dialogic process in which they can move along seeking help from people and resources including themselves, making adjustments in both their activities and cognition, and gaining new understandings of their work.

Jiaoyanzu teacher groups fit well into the sociocultural perspective as reflection with peers and the resources they bring along with them are essential in the groups' conceptualization. In the study, we explore the outcomes of teachers' reflections and engagement in these groups.

Freeman and Johnson's Tripartite Sociocultural Framework of Teacher Knowledge Base

To understand teacher knowledge base, we used Freeman and Johnson's tripartite framework (see Figure 5.1). Freeman and Johnson's (1998) tripartite framework for understanding situates teacher knowledge base in the nexus of (a) the teachers' experiences as learners; (b) the nature of schools and schooling; and (c) the nature of language teaching. The focus of "teachers as learners" includes how teachers' prior knowledge, beliefs, and training inform their current instructional practices. It also focuses on teachers as learners of teaching. The nature of schools and schooling refers, respectively, to synchronic and diachronic influences of teachers' experiences in schools and communities and how their learning unfolds over short and long periods of time (Freeman, 2009, p. 16) in those contexts. As integral members of their communities, teachers understand not just their immediate physical and sociocultural settings but also deeply embedded elements such as underlying values and hidden curricula that are developed and held over time. The third domain of the framework is predicated on teachers' understanding of learners and learning processes in their own classrooms which, however, cannot "be separated from the teacher as a learner and from the contexts in which teaching is done" (Freeman & Johnson, 1998, p. 410). The knowledge does not only have relevance to teachers' immediate situation but renders itself as part of the informational gathering process that helps teachers to theorize about teaching on a more general scale. This is a perspective that sees teaching and learning as intertwined and informing each other. When teachers see "teaching as learning and learning as teaching" (Branscombe, Goswami & Schwartz cited in Cochran-Smith & Lytle, 1999, p. 281), they see their classrooms more than a place for application: it is a place for learning (Freeman, 2009, p. 14).

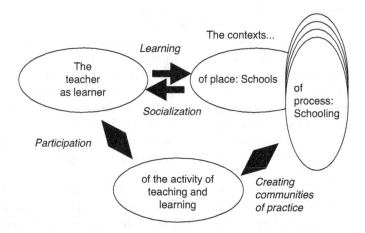

FIGURE 5.1 Freeman and Johnson's (1998) Tripartite Framework

Research Question

The main research question we investigated in the study is that given the prevalence of the jiaoyanzu in the Chinese English language teachers' lives, what are the aspects/sources of teacher knowledge that can be identified when teachers reflected with members of the jiaoyanzu in comparison to when they reflected individually?

Method

We undertook a mixed method approach to our research in which we combined quantitative and qualitative approaches. Our questions were translated into Mandarin and teachers responded in a mixture of Mandarin and English. Before we investigated the two research questions, we first surveyed the thirty Chinese English language teachers in the middle and high schools we worked in and obtained descriptive statistics from teachers on their perceptions of the nature and the importance of working and reflecting together with jiaoyanzu members. The survey asked teachers to rank the reasons why collaborating with the jiaoyanzu peers were important. (See Table 5.3 for findings.) The information helped us to contextualize our findings within this collaborative system that is unique to Chinese teachers. The return rate to our survey was 92 percent or twenty-eight out of thirty respondents.

Our qualitative approach is defined by the analysis of five teachers' stimulated recalls (SRs) (both verbal and written) of their videotaped teaching with peers and by themselves. (See Table 5.1 for the description of the teachers.)

The approach is most suited to probe teachers' thinking behind the teaching segment that is being replayed during the SRs. We facilitated the reflection with the following general questions, namely:

- What new information did you obtain about your lesson after you completed the peer- and self-reflections? As you reflected with your peers and by yourself, did your lesson happen the way you wanted it to happen?
- What did you learn about your teaching and yourself as a teacher through the peer- and self-reflections?

TABLE 5.1 Teacher Demographic Chart

	Age	*Grade level*	*Teaching years*
Laoshi Li	31	Elementary	8 years
Laoshi Fang	52	Elementary	13 years
Laoshi Xi	42	Middle	20 years
Laoshi Wen	33	High School	10 years
Laoshi Zhong	52	High School	30 years

Data Collection

We conducted the data collection in two phases. In Phase 1, each teacher was videotaped teaching for about 30–40 minutes, after which she met with two colleagues (a teaching peer and a senior colleague/administrator) to watch and discuss the video clip. In Phase 2, the teachers were given a hyperlink to their teaching video clips and/or DVDs of their teaching to reflect on alone at home. In both instances, the teachers then reported their reflections in writing and verbally to the researchers. The teachers took anywhere from two to five days to complete the reports on their reflections. Thus the sources of data for the study are as follows:

- Survey results on the importance of teacher collaboration;
- Teachers' written reports on their reflections with peers;
- Teachers' discussions with researchers regarding peer-reflection reports (transcribed);
- Teachers' written report on their self-reflections vis-à-vis the videotaped teaching;
- Teachers' discussions with researchers regarding self-reflection reports (transcribed).

Data Coding and Analysis

Data was analyzed by three coders using descriptive statistics and analytical themes. The survey provided descriptive statistics on the importance of the jiaoyanzu. The results were tabulated from a Likert scale that ranged from the "Most Important" to the "Least Important" reasons for working and learning with peers in the jiaoyanzu. (See Table 5.2 for findings.)

The coders analyzed the data for the first and second questions using the thematic approach. A theme is a pattern emerging in response to the research questions asked and it carries meaning within the data set we obtained (Braun & Clarke, 2006). The coders took the analytic approach in identifying themes in

TABLE 5.2 Collaboration Motivation

Reasons for collaboration	Likert Scale Most Important Least Important 1 2 3 4 5
Additional resources	37.2 ranked 2 and above
Friendship with colleagues	20.1 ranked 2 and above
Students' achievement	18.6 ranked 2 and above
Additional training	15.5 ranked 2 and above
School rules	9.9 ranked 2 and above

that they looked at the data through the lenses of Freeman and Johnson's teacher knowledge base. As units of analysis, the coders focused on speech segments. According to Henri and Rigault (1996), a speech segment is defined as "the smallest unit of delivery linked to a single theme, directed at the same addressee (all, individual, subgroup), identified by a single type (illocutionary act), having a single function (focus)" (p. 62).

Disagreements among the coders led to the narrowing, expansion, and/or elimination of themes (Miles & Huberman, 1994, p. 64). Inter-rater reliability was 91.1 percent, based on the ratio of agreements to total agreements and disagreements.

Findings and Discussions

We started the research with a survey that provided a context for the findings directly related to the research question. The survey findings are summarized in Table 5.2. Most surprising to us was that "friendship with colleagues" emerged as a significant reason for working together in the jiaoyanzu groups. Because jiaoyanzu teacher groups are mandated, we had expected "mandated school rules" to be the powerful external motivator, but in fact they were ranked the lowest. Thus, despite the mandate, sustaining interpersonal relationships prevailed as a reason for working together in the jiaoyanzu groups over authoritarian directives. Trusting relationships and sense of interdependency fostered by the jiaoyanzu may have empowered the teachers to work together despite having limited influence in changing school rules.

> We are always seeking to get into the same office quickly so that we could exchange our opinions every day, every minute, if we work together. We come together and discuss what we are going to teach and how we are going to do this, and then we share the teaching load so that we can finish our unit . . . We pass lesson plans around so that everybody can share and learn. This time the experienced teachers wrote three lesson plans, next the younger teachers will prepare three classes. Everybody is supposed to do that. . . . We can't change what we are told to do but we can help each other.
> *(Wen Laoshi, stimulus recall interview, June 19, 2011)*

Sztompka's (1998) argument was that power from the top disrupts collaboration through the arbitrary imposition of rules which then leads to trust diminishing between colleagues. However, our survey findings show that when a mandate from the top is not arbitrary but instead coincides with the organic ways that teachers work, it becomes incidental as it is subsumed by the teachers' regular activities. Administrators who thus pay attention to how their teachers conduct their activities and provide directives that are in line with what is already in place will find teacher support for their initiatives and undertakings.

TABLE 5.3 Most Frequently Identified Themes and Focus Areas

Freeman and Johnson's Framework	*Peer-reflections themes*	*No. of statements out of 617*	*Self-reflections themes*	*No. of statements out of 274*
• Knowledge gained from reflecting on teachers' experiences as learners	• Content • Working with peers • Research-based information	72 statements (11.6%)	• Content • Research-based information • Historical information	29 statements (10.58%)
• Knowledge gained from schools and schooling contexts	• Pressures from school, district, national exams • Difficulties with students' diverse backgrounds • Limited use or availability of English in immediate environment	79 statements (12.8%)	• Pressures from school, district, national exams • Teachers' many roles in school • Overwork	45 statements (16.42%)
• Knowledge gained from classroom teaching and learning	• What students liked • Students' struggles • Task-based teaching	136 statements (22.04%)	• What students liked • Things to do next time • Teaching mannerisms	31 statements (11.3%)

Given this background information, the subsequent findings in the study provide a picture as to the importance Chinese ELTs place on the knowledge gained working with jiaoyanzu peers. (See Table 5.3.)

In terms of the question of knowledge that emerged when teachers reflected with their peers, analysis of written reports and transcripts revealed that knowledge that emerged most significantly related to "classroom teaching and learning" (22/55 or 40%). Within this knowledge type, the top three areas of peer-based reflections (22.04% of all statements) are about "what students liked," "students' struggles," and "task-based teaching." In contrast, when the teachers undertook individual reflections, knowledge based on "contextual issues" was most frequently the point of focus (16/36 or 44.44%). In terms of self-reflections, the main areas involved knowledge derived from understanding the "outside pressures from society, school, district, national exams," "teachers' many roles in school," and from "overworking."

We include quotes from teachers reflecting with peers and when they reflected on their own. The teachers' names are prefaced with "laoshi" or teacher as they are known in the classroom. The following quotes are illustrative of some of the knowledge that emerged from discussions with peers:

"What Students Liked"

Most students like presentations in class that are close to their life, like the "Riddle." The new standards in China stress that now, real life, real life. For most students, they expect the presentation to be lively and interesting. "More fun and less knowledge," this is what the students often say! We have to think about what students are interested in always. My partner and I talked about that.

Laoshi Fang (Elementary)

"Students' Struggles"

This year I taught that third year boy, you know. He studied very hard. He reads the books, listens to the tapes and recites the words. But he cannot remember and he cannot speak English. I teach him so many times. I don't know what to do. I think he's from somewhere around Beijing or maybe he just came with his family from remote areas like Fangshan or Yangqing or from some place close. Students from there only started to learn English and they are usually from families of ordinary workers; some of them peasants.

Laoshi Li (Elementary)

"Task-Based Teaching"

Ms. Chia and I were talking about how teachers should not only rely on their experience. They should also participate in research. Task-based teaching is what we are talking about now in standards. We have research projects every two years in our group. Only in this way, can we reflect on our experience and mistakes. . . . And I think the most important part of my research experience is that it helps me in the decision-making part in the classroom.

Laoshi Zhong (High School)

In terms of individual reflections, the following quotes demonstrate teachers' awareness that their teaching is situated in the larger picture of institutional and societal infrastructure:

"Pressures"

Our teachers work so hard, very hard. It is very hard for teachers—we use most lunch times for remedial class. Some teachers go to students' home and give them extra lessons. And this is because the principal is focusing on the whole school . . . we must have the number one score for our district. It is very terrible for students and for us . . . What happens to 3% of students who cannot pass?

Laoshi Fang (Elementary)

"Teachers' Many Roles"

In my class, I shared the story of "sand and stone." If someone hurts you, write his name on the sand. The wind will blow it away and you forgive; but if someone helps you, you'd better carve his name on a rock, and remember him. . . . I share the stories like that in my class because look at what is happening in our school. Students have no one but the teachers. Our society is so busy. Parents often call me for help. All of us are busy but we must care for our students. We become many things to them. Maybe that's the most important thing.

Laoshi Xi (Middle School)

"Overworking"

In China, we always say that the teachers are just like candles. We burn ourselves out as we give light to our students. This is not a good sacrifice.

Laoshi Li (Elementary)

Using Freeman and Johnson's framework, we found that when teachers reflected together, they mainly focused on the practical aspects of classroom teaching and what they learned from events in their classrooms. This finding confirms the emphasis on technical matters often cited in teacher reflections (see Zeichner & Liston, 1987; Korthagen, 2001; Ghaye, 2011). When teachers reflected individually, on the other hand, the percentage of themes under "school and schooling context" (16.42%) was higher than those of other themes, suggesting their awareness of their work as embedded in the larger society. The data make sense contextually that when busy teachers get together to reflect, they are very task-oriented and get down to business very quickly. Additionally, when teachers are working with other individuals, there can be face-saving issues involved particularly in a high-context culture such as China where personal reputation and interpersonal relationships reign sovereign and where there can be personal risks to overt criticisms of the macro system. In contrast, when teachers are reflecting alone, there is more time and opportunity to pull back and to see the larger picture without the competing agendas of other individuals, without the worry of criticism and concern for making accessible self-revealing information to colleagues who might use the information irresponsibly.

At this early point in our work, our research has enabled us to make the argument that jiaoyanzu/peer- and self-reflections serve different but complementary roles in English language teachers' learning and professional development. While jiaoyanzu reflections are most conducive to a focus on practical matters of instruction, self-reflections lead teachers to step back and see the larger picture. We take this stance as we reflected upon our data vis-à-vis Van Manen's (1977) three levels of teaching reflection. In "technical reflection," the focus is on the efficiency of the application of educational knowledge and principles toward the attainment of specified goals; in "practical action," the concern is with clarifying assumptions underlying teaching and assessing the educational outcomes of instructional action (Zeichner & Liston, 1987); and finally, "critical reflection" targets the moral and ethical justifiability of educational practices, policies, and social infrastructure. It is a reflection that results in judgment situated in the socio-historical-politico-cultural contexts in which teaching and learning are undertaken (Hatton & Smith, 1994). In light of the teachers' quotes and in our data, we see, for example, "technical rationality" particularly evident under "Classroom and Teaching and Learning." "Critical Reflection," on the other hand, often appears under "School and Schooling Context," in which the teachers questioned the impact of circumstances in their workplace on their students' performance and the teachers' teaching and responsibilities.

Although our data do not show a precise division between the levels of reflections when teachers reflect with jiaoyanzu peers and when they reflected alone, the data do show the potential these two types of reflective settings have to yield different but valuable information. In this regard, because of the reflections' utility, professional development programs for teachers, thus, must provide opportunities in which joint and individual reflections can take place.

Our research data, however, affirm the sociocultural sources of teachers' knowledge and the information that constitutes their expertise. For us, as teachers and teacher educators, this particular sociocultural perspective is critical. It provides affirmation for the argument that teachers are actively involved in their own learning and acquisition of expertise. In this regard, teacher professional development should not start by looking at teachers as "empty vessels waiting to be filled with theoretical and pedagogical skills" (Freeman & Johnson, 1998, p. 401), rather, it should start with considering how teachers' experiences and beliefs inform and shape their teaching theory and practice. In this way, it should not start by looking at teachers as passive knowledge consumers and focusing on how well and efficiently they implement new theories, methods, or materials imposed on them; rather it should begin with engaging teachers with exploring how they can "reconstruct themselves as legitimate knowledge producers" (Shin, 2006, p. 162) and as generators and theorizers of teaching knowledge in their own right (Cochran-Smith & Lytle, 1999; Johnson, 2006). Due recognition is to be given to teacher "insider knowledge" which is not only a critical but also a most relevant component of teachers' professional development as it situates knowledge in the specific rather than hypothetical circumstances of teachers.

Implications and Conclusion

For the Chinese English language teachers with whom we work, we recognize that their jiaoyanzu peers play an important role in their professional lives. This study has affirmed to us what the Chinese English language teachers inherently know. However, our study also has informed us that in our capacity as teacher educators, we played a valuable role in inserting ourselves into the school system to create opportunities and a safe space for teachers to reflect on their own as part of the teachers' learning and development process.

In terms of our work in the U.S., our study has affirmed that the collaborative workshops we organize in the teacher development grant projects we are involved in are valuable and necessary. The workshops are the most frequently requested and positively reviewed by our participants. In addition, our study stresses the need for us to allocate time and space for individual reflective opportunities. We have done so through adding asynchronous online platforms in our workshops where our participants have time to think about and deliberate on their individual thoughts that they post online. We have also added "self-storying" components to our workshops whereby our participants share their personal connections to information they derived from working alongside with other participants and with us.

In terms of the research itself, we had some concerns that the teachers reported what they thought we expected from them. However, we feel confident in the authenticity of what we were hearing from the teachers through our efforts of triangulating information from the multiple sources of data, and through our constant presence in their schools for an extended period of time that contributed to the fostering of trust and openness of communication. Overall, this experience has strengthened our belief that teacher reflections are critical for meaningful change in how teachers develop professionally (Johnson, 2006). Along those lines, Lǎoshī Fang's reflection provides us encouragement that it may already be on the way:

> Maybe we can change the way we're teaching, not the traditional way, or maybe not the Chinese way or the American way. Maybe we can mix them together. We have to change. There is a Chinese saying, "be not afraid of changing slowly; be afraid only of standing still." My conversations with my young partner (nianqīng jiaoshī tongban) have shown me this.

Note

1. A version of this chapter was published in *Teacher Education Quarterly* (2014, volume 41, pp. 71–88).

References

Bailey, K., Curtis, A., & Nunan, D. (1998). Undeniable insights: The collaborative use of three professional development practices. *TESOL Quarterly, 32*(3), 546–556.
Braun, V., & Clarke, V. (2006). Using thematic analysis in psychology. *Qualitative Research in Psychology, 3*(2), 77–101.
Cochran-Smith, M., & Lytle, S. L. (1999). Relationships of knowledge and practice: Teacher learning in communities. *Review of Research in Education, 24,* 249–305.
Conway, P. F. (2001). Anticipatory reflection while learning to teach: From a temporally truncated to a temporally distributed model of reflection in teacher education. *Teaching and Teacher Education, 17,* 89–106.
Dewey, J. (1933). *How we think: A restatement of the relation of reflective thinking to the educative process.* New York: D. C. Heath & Co.
Fook, J., White, S., & Gardner, F. (2006). Critical reflection: A review of contemporary literature and understandings. In S. White, J. Fook & F. Gardner (Eds.), *Critical reflection in health and social care* (pp. 3–21). Maidenhead, Berks: Open University Press.
Freeman, D. (2009). The scope of second language teacher education. In A. Burns & J. C. Richards (Eds.), *The Cambridge guide to second language teacher education* (pp. 11–19). Cambridge: Cambridge University Press.
Freeman, D., & Johnson, K. E. (1998). Reconceptualizing the knowledge-base of language teacher education. *TESOL Quarterly, 32*(3), 397–417.
Ghaye, T. (2011). *Teaching and learning through reflective practice: A practical guide to positive action* (2nd ed.). New York: Routledge.
Hatton, N., & Smith, D. (1994, July 2–6). *Facilitating reflection: Issues and research.* Proceedings from the 24th Conference of the Australian Teacher Education Association, Brisbane, Queensland, Australia.
Henri, F., & Rigault, C. (1996). Collaborative distance education and computer conferencing. In T. T. Liao (Ed.), *Advanced educational technology: Research issues and future potential* (pp. 45–76). Berlin: Springer-Verlag.
Howard, T. C. (2003). Culturally relevant pedagogy: Ingredients for critical teacher reflection. *Theory Into Practice, 42,* 195–202.
John, P. D. (2002). The teacher educator's experience: Case studies of practical professional knowledge. *Teaching and Teacher Education, 18,* 323–341.
Johnson, K. E. (2006). The sociocultural turn and its challenges for second language teacher education. *TESOL Quarterly, 40*(1), 235–257.
Johnson, K. E., & Golombek, P. R. (2003). Seeing teacher learning. *TESOL Quarterly, 37*(4), 729–737.
Korthagen, F. A. J. (2001). *Linking practice and theory: The pedagogy of realistic teacher education.* Mahwah, NJ: Lawrence Erlbaum Associates, Inc.
Kyriacou, C. (1994). Reflective teaching in a wider context. In A. Peck & D. Westgate (Eds.), *Language teaching in the mirror: Reflections on Practice* (pp. 3–8). London: Center for Information on Language Teaching and Research.
Langer, E. J. (1997). *The power of mindful learning.* Reading, MA: Addison-Wesley Publishing.
Loughran, J. J. (1996). *Developing reflective practice: Learning about teaching and learning through modeling.* Washington, DC: Falmer Press.
Marcos, J. J. M., & Tillema, H. (2006). Studying studies on teacher reflection and action: A appraisal of research contributions. *Educational Research Review, 1,* 112–132.

Meijer, P. C., Zanting, A., & Verloop, N. (2002). How can student teachers elicit experienced teachers' practical knowledge? Tools, suggestions, and significance. *Journal of Teacher Education, 53*(5), 406–419.

Mezirow, J. (1991). *Transformative dimensions of adult learning.* San Francisco, CA: Jossey-Bass.

Miles, M. B., & Huberman, A. M. Z. (1994). *Qualitative data analysis: A sourcebook of new methods.* Newbury Park, CA: Sage.

Paine, L. W. (1990). The teacher as virtuoso: A Chinese model of teaching. *Teachers College Record, 93*(1), 49–81.

Peck, A., & Westgate, D. (Eds.). (1994). *Language teaching in the mirror: Reflections on practice.* London: Center for Information on Language Teaching and Research.

Rogers, R. R. (2001). Reflections in higher education: A concept analysis. *Innovative Higher Education, 26*(1), 37–57.

Schön, D. A. (1983). *The reflective practitioner: How professionals think in action.* New York: Basic Books.

Shin, H. (2006). Rethinking TESOL from a SOL's perspective: Indigenous epistemology and decolonizing praxis in TESOL. *Critical Inquiry in Language Studies, 3*(1), 147–167.

Smith, K. (2005). Teacher educator's expertise: What do novice teachers and teachers educators say? *Teaching and Teacher Education, 21*, 177–192.

Sztompka, P. (1998). Trust, distrust and two paradoxes of democracy. *European Journal of Social Theory, 1*(19), 19–32.

Van Manen, M. (1977). Linking ways of knowing with ways of being practical. *Curriculum Inquiry, 6*, 205–228.

Vygotsky, L. S. (1978). *Mind in society: The development of higher mental processes.* Cambridge, MA: Harvard University Press.

Zeichner, K. M., & Liston, D. P. (1987). Teaching student teachers to reflect. *Harvard Educational Review, 57*(1), 23–48.

6

HIGH-STAKES PUBLIC TEACHING COMPETITIONS

Failure Is Not Falling but Failure Is Not Getting up From Each Fall

Faridah Pawan

Introduction

For Chinese English language teachers under forty years of age, teacher competitions are a regular occurrence. Audience members consist of fellow teachers, administrators, teacher leaders, officials, and other interested parties. In the competitions, teachers are assigned to teach students that the teachers meet a few days before or right before competitions. A phalanx of judges evaluates the competition by observing the teaching itself and by assessing teachers' responses to judges' questions immediately following each teaching session. The competitions are intense and the stakes are high because success in the competitions can lead to promotion and job security for the teachers. It will also mean an enhancement in the reputation for their mentors, school administrators, and school districts. If teachers win at national competitions, even their provinces benefit from increased visibility and, consequently, increased funding.

Information regarding the competitions described in this chapter is derived from interviews and observations of thirty-two teachers across three competitions in two districts in the north and northwest of Beijing. Fifteen judges were also interviewed during deliberation sessions. Materials they developed for the competitions were also collected and analyzed. In addition, information was derived from numerous open classes and demonstrations of teaching from the competitors in their own schools in preparation for the competitions.

Competition as a Paradox

High-stakes teacher competitions where individuals are rewarded for their teaching excellence, while common, are contrary to the long-held Chinese values of "collectivism" and egalitarianism among peers. A reminder of the latter is the

Chinese proverb, "the first bird to fly away from the flock is the first bird shot" (枪打出头鸟, qiang da chu tou niao). In this sense, individual achievement is seen with unkind regard. However, in the context of schools, it can perhaps be understood within the ideal context of "guanxi" (关系), in which individual achievement is seen as only possible if there is mutual support and collaboration between people in a tight and well-connected community. In guanxi, emotional closeness comes from the feeling of a sense of interdependence and the ability to mutually benefit from knowing and helping each other (Zhuang, Xi & Tsang, 2010). These interactive and collaborative behaviors, as Lee and Dawes (2005) point out, are based on "renqing" (人情) and "mianzi" (面子). It can be interpreted as a "favor debt" in which the former (renqing) is the provision of assistance to others and the latter (mianzi) is the expected return of the extended favor. It feeds into the spirit of collectivism whereby everyone works together for the collective good but no one stands to benefit alone. Such a collaborative and cooperative relationship underlies the establishment of a supportive lifelong network for all individuals. It is the basis of what is known as the Chinese "courtyard" (四合院, siheyuan) culture. For it to be sustained, there ideally needs to be respect, humility, and the willingness from everyone to work together to support each other when the need arises.

Faure and Fang's (2008) explanation of the "Yin and Yang" (black and white) bipolarization in Chinese culture provides another context for understanding the paradox between individual excellence and communal good. They explain that opposite values are not in opposition with one another but rather, they co-exist, even though at times, uncomfortably with each other. Yin represents the energies and forces of moon, water, dark, passivity, and femininity, and Yang, that of the sun, fire, light, activity, and masculinity. In this regard, in China, the paradoxes illustrate competing forces that co-exist with each other, such as those shown in Table 6.1.

TABLE 6.1 Paradoxical Chinese Values (Adapted from Faure and Fang, 2008, p. 196)

Paradoxical Chinese values		
1. Guanxi	vs.	Professionalism
2. Importance of face	vs.	Self-expression and directness
3. Thrift	vs.	Materialism and ostentatious consumption
4. Family and group orientation	vs.	Individuation
5. Aversion to law	vs.	Respect for legal practices
6. Respect for etiquette, age, hierarchy	vs.	Respect for simplicity, creativity, and competence
7. Long-term orientation	vs.	Short-term orientation
8. Traditional creeds	vs.	Modern approaches

These contradictory forces co-exist currently in China in the midst of its rapid social and economic change. When one asks people on the street what is happening in their nation, an expression likely to be heard is "ri xin yue yi" (日新月异) or "things are changing day by day." In other words, the course of the future is constantly changing. In daily life, it is quite evident, for example, in the streets of Beijing where each day a new construction site emerges, a new street is being built, new policies are announced, or a new factory opens. Despite and because of these changes, Faure and Fang (2008) assert that the Chinese hold onto one of its most important cultural characteristics, that is, "the ability to manage paradoxes" (p. 196) and bring balance and harmony (Faure and Fang, 2008, p. 195) to the community. Thus, despite the individual-centeredness of the teaching competitions, these competitions are valued because of their perceived benefits for the reputation of the group as a whole in the wider education community.

Teacher Excellence as a Concept

In her seminal article, Paine (1990) describes the Chinese model for teaching as that of the virtuoso (p. 54). Excellent teachers are artists who have mastered their craft through a combination of their mastery of the subject matter, their well-researched interpretation of information from it, and finally, their communication of the information to students in explicit and organized ways that are aligned with students' interests, multiple levels of understanding and abilities. In undertaking the job, teachers undertake learning and understanding content, solidifying the understanding, and finding applications and means to deliver them to students so that its relevance and use is apparent. Excellent teachers are thus likened to a virtuoso performer on stage with the students as their rapt audience ready to absorb and benefit from the information the teachers provide.

It is clear that there are definite structural stages, organizational steps, and functional tools to achieve all these ends, but as Paine points out, teaching for Chinese teachers is "not simply technical wizardry but also about heart" (p. 54). This is evident from what is said by a veteran teacher interviewed for this chapter, who was one of the judges in a teaching competition:

> To be a good teacher, you have to be very close to students. When you want students to like your class they have to love you. I need to show students I care and love them and when they know this, they are happy and I can feel I am a good teacher. When I go back to my English office, I share with my young colleagues about this happiness in my teaching. I want them to know it and to know that you have to think with your heart when you teach.
>
> *(Ms. Hao, 51, elementary school teacher for 30 years and a judge for 8 years)*

The teacher is reiterating the concept of *xin* (心) or "heart," which Sun (cited in Zhang & Zhu, 2008) points out represents both mind and heart and in that regard, the non-separation between thinking and feeling in the Chinese perspective. Zhang and Zhu argue that in addition to thinking intellectually, teachers need to be able to invest emotional labor into their teaching by managing, monitoring, and regulating their emotions to enhance teaching effectiveness. The emotional aspect of teaching is alluded to in Table 6.2, where teaching competition criteria show the expectation that teachers demonstrate "love" for students.

According to Zhang and Ng's (2011) investigation, there are four principles of good teaching: (1) moral conduct, (2) competence, (3) achievement, and (4) duties. Emotion aligns with teachers' moral conduct in which teachers are able to demonstrate their devotion and connection to students. This can involve interaction in the classroom as well as outside of it to include counseling students in their offices and establishing trusting relationships with their parents. "Moral conduct" also includes teachers' responsibilities for teaching students good citizenship and making sure student behavior does not fall outside of the boundaries of good conduct and compliance to rules (see also Fan, Wang, and Chen's Chapter 3). On the other hand, "competence" and "achievement" refer to the demonstration of teaching skills including in the classroom and teaching competitions. It also refers to teachers' ability to demonstrate improvement through reflection and research on their own teaching. Excellent teachers should be able to showcase that their teaching is informed by research, evidence of which is showcased in teachers' annual merit report and/or publications in journals. Finally, teacher duties include the ability for teachers to demonstrate loyalty to their schools and other institutional structures including "their participation and collaboration in lesson preparation, classroom observation, in training programs and ad hoc tasks" (Zhang and Ng, 2011, p. 571). Excellent teachers are thus those who serve the profession comprehensively. It is thus not surprising that one of the often-cited metaphors to describe teachers' jobs is that of a "lighted candle." Teachers should be willing to give it their all in the job, as the candle metaphor suggests, and be willing to consume all of their resources in the drive to excel on behalf of their students and colleagues.

Competition Description: You Fall Down Seven Times, You Get up Eight

Teaching competitions, as mentioned in the previous sections, are a significant part of Chinese English language teachers' responsibilities in demonstrating excellence. As the following discussions will show, they require intensive preparation and teacher engagement.

TABLE 6.2 Teaching Competition Criteria

Original criteria		Direct translation of criteria	
评价项目	评价要点	Topic	Requirements
教学目标	★1. 符合课程标准（知识与能力，过程与方法，情感态度与价值观）。	Goals of teaching	★1. Fits Teaching Standards (Knowledge and skills, process and method, emotional attitude and values)
	★2. 符合学生实际，有效进行前测，照顾学生差异。		★2. Fits students' actual conditions, effectively predict, consider differences in students' abilities
教学准备	★3. 创设良好的学习环境，教学资源准备充足（适应教学目标、内容，利于学生发展）。	Preparation	★3. Creates good environment for teaching, has prepared abundant teaching resources (which fits goals of teaching, content of teaching, and is good for students' development)
教学组织与策略	★4. 教学内容的使用（合理组织教材，教学设计有梯度，具备开放性、层次性）。	Organization and tactics for teaching	★4. Use of teaching materials (organize textbooks effectively, design differently for different level of students, is open and has diverse depths)
	★5. 教学活动的设计（根据目标和内容设计科学有效的教学活动，及时捕捉生成、利用生成）。		★5. Design of teaching activities (design scientific and effective activities according to goals and content of teaching; make use of student-generated input in time)
	★6. 学习活动的指导（面向全体，重视差异，问题情境引起情趣，具有启发性）。		★6. Instructions of teaching activities (face all students, pay attention to differences (in students), scenarios of questions are fun, are inspiring)
	★7. 学习活动的调控（能根据反馈信息对教学过程、难度适时调整，能引导学生全员参与、小组合作积极动手实践）。		★7. Adjustment of and control over teaching activities (can adjust process and difficulty of teaching according to timely, feedback can instruct all students to take part, can instruct to make students work in teams and practice)
教师素质	★8. 关爱学生，尊重人格，师生关系和谐，气氛融洽。	Quality of teachers	★8. Love and take care of students, respect human rights, have harmonious relationship with students, have good environment
	★9. 教学技巧（语言准确科学，具有激励性、启发性；板书使用合理；能熟练运用现代信息技术等）		★9. Skills of teaching (use of accurate and scientific language, encouraging and inspiring; effective use of chalk board; can make good use of modern information technology)
	★10. 评价学生的方式多样，以激励为主，面向全体，关注差异。		★10. Evaluate students in diverse ways, mainly encourage them, face all students, pay attention to differences
学生参与状态	★11. 参与广度（全体参与，全程参与）。		
	★12. 参与态度（有较强的求知欲，积极主动，善于倾听、合作、分享）。		
	★13. 参与深度（勤于思考，善于思考，敢于提出问题和发表不同见解）。		

(Continued)

TABLE 6.2 (Continued)

Original criteria		Direct translation of criteria	
学习效果综评	*14. 大多数学生完成学习任务,每个学生能体验到自我发展的愉悦。	**Students' participation**	*11. Broadness (**everyone** participates **all the time**)
			*12. Attitude (have strong desire for knowledge, take active roles in learning, are good at listening, cooperating, sharing)
			*13. Depth (think often and deep, can ask questions and express different opinions)
		Effect of study	*14. Most students can accomplish study tasks, every student can experience the joy of self-development
		Conclusion	

Organization and Setting

There are multiple levels of the competitions organized by multiple agencies described by Wang (2011) in Figure 6.1. The figure also describes the levels of competition from the local school level all the way to the national level.

Each year, the competitions at each of the levels are focused on different themes and thus replication of lessons is kept to a minimum, if at all. In other words, teachers have to prepare new lessons each time they compete. The focus for lessons varies and is often determined top-down, as described in Pawan's Introduction, by national officials who are concerned with new school reform directives, district officials who are focusing on test refinement, principals with new priorities for professional development, or teacher-leaders who see the need for teachers to improve in a particular way:

> My leader gave me the work and I followed her advice. She also gave me a chart that I use in my lesson to teach the phrases in the lesson. My leader supports me very much. I have been teaching for only six years but she has been a teacher for more than twenty years. She can tell what I need to do and to get better [and to improve]. I listen to her; I have to. . . .
> (Mr. Lo, 27, secondary teacher for 5 years)

There is extensive preparation in the lead up to each level of the competition. Teachers design lessons in close collaboration with colleagues in their teacher groups or "jiaoyanzu" (教研组) consisting of six to eight individuals (see Pawan and Fan's Chapter 5). Besides leaders in the groups who direct their activities,

FIGURE 6.1 Public Lesson/Competition Organizers

there are also Backbone (骨干, gugan) Teachers whose experiences give them authority to be the central players and key advisors in the preparation. Much of the activities and discussions in the group will center on three elements in a lesson that is being prepared, namely, the knowledge points (知识点, zhishi dian), the key points (重点, zhong dian), and the difficult points (难点, nan dian) (Tsui & Wong, 2010, p. 289). These points are not determined at random but rather through research which teachers are expected to be able to show evidence of at the competitions as well.

The teachers then undertake a series of pre-competition teaching trials by conducting the lessons several times to be observed and critiqued by colleagues in their teacher groups, other teachers, and their principals. For one teacher, the preparation included eight open classes between the months of September to November:

> This lesson I can teach very well because I practiced to teach it more than eight times. Every time, I made it better to teach students to communicate, how to start a topic like giving them pictures at the beginning. My colleagues also watched me teach eight times and I learned many things from them.
>
> *(Mr. Chao, 32, secondary teacher for 4 years)*

In addition to providing feedback from observations, colleagues also attend other competitions to obtain information and to share it with the teachers in their jiaoyanzu who are also about to compete.

Each competition can take up to six to eight hours a day over a period of two to four days, depending on each district's specific circumstances. The day of the competitions is preceded by teachers submitting their lesson plans,

A. Auditorium setting with students in front, judges, right behind followed by colleagues in the back behind the judges

B. Gymnasium setting where students are in the middle, judges on the right, and colleagues all around, including behind the judges

FIGURE 6.2 Competition Settings

materials, and explanation for their lessons to five to seven judges. If timely arrangements could be made, a few days prior to the competitions, the teachers will also get to meet the students they are going to teach for brief "getting-to-know" sessions. Otherwise, the teachers will meet the students on the competition floor. The venues for the competitions vary but usually they are in a large auditorium or a gymnasium. In the latter, teachers usually set up their classrooms in a U-shape, with the students in the middle, the judges at the far end, and colleagues all around the sides and behind the judges. In well-resourced school districts, technology is extensively used to record the teaching with multiple video cameras and television screens as well as document cameras that show all the materials on the teacher competitors' desks and those they distribute to students. The teachers compete by teaching their prepared lessons for 40–50 minutes. After the lesson is over, their students leave the auditorium but the audience members and the judges remain for the evaluation.

Figure 6.2 illustrates two competition settings.

Evaluation

The five to seven judges consist of senior teachers who have received multiple awards themselves. Although there are slight variations from one competition to another, judges typically look for teachers' ability to: (1) technically apply knowledge and curriculum principles toward lesson objectives, and (2) clarify and explain how the lessons objectives are met. Table 6.2 provides an example of the criteria used by judges from one of the competitions.

The two-step process of evaluation begins with teachers being judged on their application of what they know and are able to do to achieve the goals. For example, they are judged on how they are able to provide and use sufficient and diverse materials, organize and control teaching strategies, deliver information, and engage students. Second, upon the completion of the lesson and departure of students from the competition floor, teachers are then expected to explain the framework, the rationale, and the research underlying their lessons.

Teachers then review their applications with the judges who engage them in a question-and-answer and critique period in the presence of their colleagues for about fifteen to thirty minutes. For one teacher, the judges' questions were as follows:

- We are not clear on one or two details in the middle of your lesson. Why did you lead students through that practice?
- The way you taught in the lesson is not the same as the lesson plan you handed in. Why?
- Explain your theory behind this lesson. What methods are you following?

After the teaching competitions, there is a third and informal stage in the evaluation that takes place in closed rooms. These sessions have to be conducted carefully as the judges can also be former or current mentors of competing teachers.

Discussions during the judges' deliberations often provide insight into the values that underpin their ideas of what makes a teacher effective. For example, for one judge, humility was a point of consideration:

> I have seen many teachers really qualified to be English teachers. Their English is very good but we do not want teachers to just to show off. I can see it in one of the teachers. What's the point?
> *(Ms. Gong, 52, middle school teacher for 23 years and a judge for 4 years)*

Another judge focused on the appropriateness of using certain words (which in this case was the English word, "should") in relation to Chinese social norms and etiquette:

> I am confused by the advice on "should" the teacher was giving to students. Why did she advise them to use that? Who is the advice appropriate for? Would it be polite to give such advice to our grandparents for example? We don't talk to grandparents that way.
> Maybe I don't see clearly what the teacher wants to say.
> *(Mr. Ma, 49, middle school teacher for 26 years and a judge for 6 years)*

As can be seen above, the judges' values and beliefs creep into their evaluations of teaching irrespective of what the official judging criteria may be. Nevertheless, because the values and beliefs were present in the judges' discussions suggests that the judges' sense of responsibility in making well-thought-out decisions was made in the context of not only the competition criteria but also by their awareness of personal and cultural factors salient to them as individuals and as members of their social group.

Outcomes

Why are the stakes so high in teaching competitions? All the interviewees provided reasons that coincide with that of Zhang and Ng's (2011), namely, achievement of honor, professional development, and monetary awards. Top rankings in competitions for teachers can lead to their promotion as senior teachers. Promotions are not easy to come by and can take a long time to achieve, as evidenced by a teacher who has taught for seventeen years of which eleven were in teaching English. However, even then he felt that he was only at a starting point:

> I am still a beginner. It is hard for me to go to advanced. You have to win a lot of competitions. I am not diligent because I am busy with daily tasks. I do not have time to seek feedback for my teaching. But for this competition, I have to do that.
>
> *(Mr. Chen, 35, secondary school teacher for 17 years)*

Thus, this lengthy and arduous period needed to advance is commonplace as it has taken more than twenty years for one of the judges to be in the senior position she currently has:

> I did several open classes and then I went to a final competition in Beijing city. I got first prize in Beijing. After that I had more chances to compete and I won a lot of competitions, the last one, a first prize in all of China. . . . I do not know how many awards I have but maybe twenty but that is over twenty years. . . . No, more than twenty.
>
> *(Ms. Peng, 51, secondary school teacher for 25 years)*

The chances of winning competitions are improved through the collective efforts of one's colleagues. The chances to compete are based on colleagues' estimation of teachers' readiness and their recommendation for the latter to compete. Thus, colleagues also have an investment in the success of their fellow teachers since individual teacher rankings also contribute to the ranking of the larger units that the teachers belong to, such as citations for being an outstanding department (school level), advanced school department in teaching (district level), and advanced subject department in research (district level) (Zhang & Ng, 2011, p. 572).

Teachers generally feel that competitions are indeed worthwhile learning and professional development opportunities for those who take part in them. Wang (2011) reported from her study of 1,600 secondary school English language teachers (ELTs) over two years (2005–2007) that almost 90 percent of them reported that teaching competitions were worthwhile, and more than half (63%) expressed a continued need for competitions to support their learning and professional development. In the same set of studies, Wang reported the following benefits that teachers gained from the competitions including opportunities:

- To see theory in practice;
- To showcase and develop competence;
- To obtain and update resources; and
- To collaborate with fellow teachers, teacher educators, curriculum experts, and educational administrators in improving instruction.

Finally, there are also financial rewards from the competition, albeit limited. Zhang and Ng (2011) describe the financial rewards for teachers from competitions can be anywhere from 100 RMB to 500 RMB (approximately U.S. $16–75) that could be sustained over several months in some cases. Given that the beginning salary for teachers is about 2,000 RMB (approximately U.S. $300 a month), these are not insignificant amounts. Nevertheless, the financial reward is almost beside the point, as competitions are stepping stones to greater goals:

> More money . . . I don't know, maybe. It is important that I win. It is an honor for our school. It is an honor for me too.
>
> *(Ms. Hsieh, 25, elementary school teacher for 3 years)*

The competitions, however, were also "mixed blessings" to the teachers interviewed. For example, in terms of putting theory into practice and showcasing competence, one teacher had the following to say:

> I feel very terrible. I do not like to take part in it but I must. I am nervous. So many people are looking at me. I do have not enough time to prepare. But I want to show the judges I can teach students to communicate what they do every day. This is the new theory to teach English.
>
> *(Ms. Tan, 25, elementary teacher for 4 years)*

For one teacher, competitions are indeed stressful but the resources and ideas gained from going through them made them worthwhile:

> I don't have benefits from the competition. I benefit nothing I think. But during practice, I get good information but the competition is stressful. From the preparations for the competition, I know more methods and

class activities and more fun activities. I look for fun activities. If students have interest, they learn more. If they hate the class, they don't want to learn. I find ways to keep English learning interesting for 3rd graders and 6th graders.

(Mr. Hung, 30, elementary school teacher for 7 years)

The competitions are mandated activities for young teachers and this is a responsibility they have to fulfill. However, the competitions allow for them to obtain peer input into their teaching and was the primary motivation for the teacher quoted here to participate despite her reservations:

Choice? No, not a choice. Everybody is supposed to do it. It is part of the job. . . . [I]t is a torture but after this kind of torture, indeed you can learn something. Everybody is there to help you. . . . The judges are scary but they say something that I think about more later.

(Ms. Lyu, 27, elementary school teacher for 5 years)

The quotes demonstrate teacher positions at both ends of the spectrum where teaching competitions are concerned. Nevertheless, since they are a significant part of the teachers' lives and their professional development efforts, a critical look at the competitions is warranted.

A Critical Look at Teaching Competitions

Teaching is a nurturing and caring profession (Noddings, 1996). It is based on relationships between caring individuals (teachers) and those cared for (students) (p. 161). Such relationships require time for trust to develop, time to monitor its effects, and time to adjust and change accordingly. In this regard, teachers do not have a causal relationship with students but they have a relationship of influence (Johnson, 2006) whereby teachers do not cause students to succeed but they influence them with sustained guidance and support toward success over time.

Teaching competitions run counter to this professional percept of teaching as a long-term endeavor. As in all competitive settings, competitions induce the achievement of short-term performance goals rather than learning goals (Lam, Yim, Law & Cheung, 2004). In the former, individuals aim to gain positive evaluations of their abilities and to outperform others. In the latter, the aim is to achieve new understandings that could lead to the refinement of old and the acquisition of new skills, respectively. In this regard, Lam et al.'s (2004) study cast doubt on the claim that teaching competitions lead to teaching excellence. They found that individuals who are under pressure to outperform others in competitive settings avoid optimal challenges and learning opportunities particularly when faced with difficulties. This means that teachers, under the pressure of competition, focus on and showcase the most accessible, solvable, and obvious instructional issues rather than delving into complexities for which there are no quick and immediate solutions that the public can see.

Intrinsic motivation is also compromised as these individuals "give an external locus of causality for their learning . . . [l]earning is no longer a task with intrinsic value" (Lam et al., 2004, p. 292). Rather than enhancing motivation, competitions undermine it as they are seen as an obligation that teachers are forced to take part in and that address criteria and external ends that they have no control over. The following teacher quote reiterates the situation:

> They (the judges) ask you to do something but I do not even look at the evaluation criteria because I don't care. Sometimes I do not understand what they think. They have different rules. I just take part because I do what the principal wants me to do.
> *(Ms. Li, 29, elementary teacher for 5 years)*

Disdain for competitions is clear in the preceding quote which echoes Paine's (1990) criticism of "teaching as a performance" concept in traditional Chinese teaching models. It is a model whereby teachers are performing to an audience who are not a part of their daily teaching lives. How their performances change the teachers' learning and, more important, that of their own students is unclear given that the task and setting are artificial:

> We prefer to teach a real class, not this kind of presenting. It is not helpful. In a real class, my colleagues can listen to me and we can help each other. It will save me a lot of time and energy. This is all not real.
> *(Ms. Pu, 28, elementary teacher for 5 years)*

It needs to be mentioned here that beyond the competitions, Chinese teachers do undertake many demonstration classes where they invite others to visit and critique them as well. Nevertheless, these "demo" classes can evolve into competition classes, and the frequency by which teachers have to undertake them not only interrupts the instructional day but can also put a heavy burden on the teachers:

> In about 4 months, I will compete again, I am afraid. I spend lots of time on the competitions and showing my lessons. It is very hard. I want to share time with my family. When I have competitions . . . almost every day, every weekend for 2 months, I am working on my lessons. Too much!
> *(Mr. Xi, 31, secondary teacher for 7 years)*

One of the reasons the preparations take such a long time relates to one of the strongest aspects of the competitions: They engage teachers in putting "Action Research" into their teaching. Action Research is a cyclical process of teachers posing questions about their lessons to themselves, to colleagues, and to students;

gathering data, analyzing and reflecting on the data; and consequently deciding on the next course of action (Ferrance, 2000). When Action Research is done well, it engages teachers in multiple and continuous cycles of research that is systematic and grounded in their realities. However, what diminishes the full beneficial effects of such a research undertaking, as can be seen from Ms. Li's quote, is that in competitions, effectiveness is evaluated on the one instance (usually after teachers give tests), on a topic that did not emerge out of their own teaching, and on the basis of external criteria rather that of the teachers' themselves.

The expression, "the old guiding the novice" (老带新, lao dai xin), is used to describe the relationship between experienced and new teachers in China. The tight collaboration that exists between them in schools through teacher groups (jiaoyanzu) is discussed at length in Pawan and Fan's Chapter 5. This collaboration is central in preparing for teaching competitions:

> My supervisor, Ms. Zhao, I listen to her and to her lessons. Ms. Zhao will tell me what to teach in the competition, in which unit, and what to prepare. She goes to my lessons and she tells me where the problems and the good points are. I also sometimes rely on other teachers but I talk to Ms. Zhao more. Also, she gives me inspirations on how to deal with problems in my competition lesson.
>
> *(Ms. Chen, 26, middle school teacher for 4 years)*

This collaboration, however, is not based on an equal relationship. As is described in the quote, young teachers spend a lot of time watching their experienced mentors teach as the more experienced teachers are considered models for good teaching. In this tightly bound relationship, victory and defeat have added dimensions in that if teachers win, then glory is shared with their mentors. However, if they do not win a competition, both teachers and mentors lose face. As such, the interdependence and the intertwining of their fates between young teachers and their mentors make the former vulnerable to control and may also limit their capacity to innovate on their own (Paine & Ma, 1993). A quote from one of the judges during the judging deliberation period makes this point quite apparent:

> No matter how good a teacher is in English, the best way to learn the language is to follow native speakers on tape and after that, the teacher can repeat. This is what the teacher leader said to the teacher we just saw. Maybe the teacher thought she did not need the tape. We are teaching a foreign language we need to have native speaker models. But she did not follow her leader's advice—that is the problem.
>
> *(Ms. Mao, 48, elementary teacher for 24 years and a judge for 10 years)*

This quote illustrates that, to this judge, the teacher in question erred by not following the advice of her mentor. Could the judge's expectation perpetuate, in the mind of the teacher who was competing, a preference for conformity to standard practices and obeisance to experienced teachers' opinions? The quote certainly suggests that to be the case.

Situating the Next Steps

It is clear from this chapter that although the competitions are common practice amongst Chinese English language teachers (ELTs), there is consternation amongst those interviewed about them. Wang (2011) suggests the alternative of using the competitions as public platforms for learning rather than as contests. She suggests, for example, that the competition lessons become a means to develop leadership and team-building skills; to share and reflect on good practices; to build teaching resources; to collaborate on joint studies of curricula, textbooks, and student needs. In other words, instead of a means to distinguish losers and winners, Wang's model conceives teaching competitions as means to expand the professional development opportunities for teachers and their professional communities.

Wang's suggestion coincides with Papert's (1986) view of "constructionism" in that learning is most meaningful when learners are engaged in learning that is real as well as pursued in a publicly shareable space such as in the teaching competitions. However, unlike in the competitions, there is no judgment involved. Creating opportunities for teachers to publicly share and deconstruct jointly their lessons empowers them to "connect with everything they know, feel, and wonder, stretching themselves into learning new things" (Martinez, 2016, para. 8). These public spaces can be informal and even virtual such as Personal Learning Networks (PLNs) where teachers, using social media, can share ideas and resources and collaborate with one another through the online medium. The aim of PLNs is the unlimited interconnection and free exchanges of ideas with colleagues. The public spaces can be formalized through disciplinary-sanctioned means as well. In 2003, Sharkey and Johnson, for example, compiled expert-teacher dialogues in the field's flagship journal, *TESOL Quarterly*, into an edited volume. In it experts' and teachers' exchanges on their understanding and use of theory and practice are published and thus legitimized as core bodies of pedagogical knowledge. In both cases, the public spaces engage teachers in collaborative sharing, understanding, and creativity.

This type of collegial support and sharing of ideas *does* exist in various forms amongst Chinese teachers. However, teaching competitions shift the focus away from collaboration toward winning and outperforming colleagues.

References

Faure, G. O., & Fang, T. (2008). Changing Chinese values: Keeping up with paradoxes. *International Business Review, 17*(2), 194–207.

Ferrance, E. (2000). *Action research.* Providence, RI: Brown University, Northeast and Islands Regional Educational Laboratory.

Johnson, K. E. (2006). The socio-cultural turn and its challenges for second language teacher education. *TESOL Quarterly*, *40*(1), 235–257.
Lam, S. F., Yim, P. S., Law, J. S., & Cheung, R. W. (2004). The effects of competition on achievement motivation in Chinese classrooms. *British Journal of Educational Psychology*, *74*(2), 281–296.
Lee, D. Y., & Dawes, P. L. (2005). Guanxi, trust, and long-term orientation in Chinese business markets. *Journal of International Marketing*, *13*(2), 28–56.
Martinez, S. (2016). *The maker movement: Standing on the shoulders of giants to own the future*. Retrieved from www.edutopia.org/blog/maker-movement-shoulders-of-giants-sylvia-martinez
Noddings, N. (1996). The caring professional. In S. Gordon, P. Benner & N. Noddings (Eds.), *Caregiving: Readings in knowledge, practice, ethics, and politics* (pp. 160–172). Philadelphia: University of Pennsylvania Press.
Paine, L. (1990). The teacher as virtuoso: A Chinese model for teaching. *The Teachers College Record*, *92*(1), 49–81.
Paine, L., & Ma, L. (1993). Teachers working together: A dialogue on organizational and cultural perspectives of Chinese teachers. *International Journal of Educational Research*, *19*(8), 675–697.
Papert, S. (1986). *Constructionism: A new opportunity for elementary science education*. Cambridge: Massachusetts Institute of Technology, Media Laboratory, Epistemology and Learning Group.
Sharkey, J., & Johnson, K. E. (Eds.). (2003). *The TESOL Quarterly dialogues: Rethinking issues of language, culture, and power*. Alexandria, VA: TESOL.
Tsui, A. B., & Wong, J. L. (2010). In search of a third space: Teacher development in mainland China. In C.K.K. Chan & N. Rao (Eds.), *Revisiting the Chinese learner* (pp. 281–311). Hong Kong: Springer/University of Hong Kong, Comparative Education Research Centre.
Wang, Q. (2011, June 10). *Making a virtue of public lessons for enhancing teacher learning in the process of curriculum change*. Proceedings from TESOL Symposium, Beijing Normal University, Beijing, China.
Zhang, X. F., & Ng, H. M. (2011). A case study of teacher appraisal in Shanghai, China: In relation to teacher professional development. *Asia Pacific Education Review*, *12*(4), 569–580.
Zhang, Q., & Zhu, W. (2008). Exploring emotion in teaching: Emotional labor, burnout, and satisfaction in Chinese higher education. *Communication Education*, *57*(1), 105–122.
Zhuang, G., Xi, Y., & Tsang, A. S. (2010). Power, conflict, and cooperation: The impact of guanxi in Chinese marketing channels. *Industrial Marketing Management*, *39*(1), 137–149.

7

THE NATIONAL GUO PEI PROJECT FOR RURAL TEACHERS

Opening Doors So That Others May Enter

Miao Pei and Wei Jin

Introduction

There have been three stages in the history of teacher training in China that involve teachers in the entire nation including English language teachers in the rural areas. The three stages align with the three teacher policies mentioned in Pei, Pawan, and Jin's Chapter 1. They can be referred to as the "diploma complimentary stage" (from 1970s to the end of 1980s), the "co-existence of diploma complimentary and continuing professional development stage" (in the 1990s), and the "continuing professional stage" (after 2000) (Li, Wu & Xu, 2006, p. 71). The first stage is a directive for employed teachers to work toward a teaching diploma through Adult Education departments at universities or colleges (教师进修学校, or jiaoshi jinxiu xuexiao). The second stage signifies that even with the diploma, teachers need to continue to pursue professional development to sustain their expertise. Finally, the third stage formalizes the requirement that teachers obtain degrees from teacher training institutions. Following the degree, teachers must pass certification examinations before they can be fully employed in schools (see Fan, Wang, and Chen's Chapter 3). As to the latest certification reform along with the Chinese government's issuance of the New Curriculum Reform in 2011, there is now an intense focus on helping to continuously update their teaching methods to adapt to students' new learning styles.

The Guo Pei Plan (国培计划, National-Level Training Plan) was developed to assist rural English teachers (RETs) in engaging in the reforms. In this chapter, we will provide an overview of the Guo Pei Plan, including the central programmatic frameworks on which it is based, the successes and challenges of programs that emerged from the plan, and our suggestions on the next steps.

The Beginnings of the Guo Pei (国培) National-Level Training Plan

Rural areas make up a large proportion of the country's territory. Many of these regions are on the western and inland part of the country and in ethnically diverse areas. They include such areas as the Inner Mongolia Autonomous Region, Guangxi Zhuang Autonomous Region, Tibet Autonomous Region, Ningxia Hui Autonomous Region, and Xingjian Uygur Autonomous Region. Specifically, according to the Sixth National Population Census survey, 50.32 percent of the population, that is, 674,149,546 people are from rural areas in China (National Bureau of Statistics, P.R.C., 2011). Because of the vastness of the areas and the monumental number of people involved, it is difficult for resources to be delivered and to reach them. Hence, it is not surprising that in the 1990s, there were rarely, if any, professional development programs for primary and secondary English language teachers in those rural areas (Li, 2010).

The lack of professional development opportunities thus translates into the lack of professionally trained English language teachers. To make up for the shortage, a common practice had been the recruitment of college students from those areas who showed promise in their achievements in the English language. Another common practice was to abscond teachers from other subject areas to teach English (see also Fan's Chapter 4). In both instances, these individuals struggled with their new teaching responsibilities because they lacked training in teaching and in the subject area itself. This was the experience of the second author of this chapter (Wei Jin), who in 1997, was taught by a teacher of such background in his hometown in a rural area in a central province in China:

> My first English teacher did not major in English. She was actually a teacher of politics and geography. My teacher was assigned to teach English because it was believed that she picked up enough of the language from her teachers in college who were English majors. She tried to teach English but that was not her strength.
>
> *(W. Jin, personal communication, September 7, 2016)*

Obviously, these attempts to solve the teacher shortage problems were inadequate and particularly difficult to resolve as the problems are part of a larger issue of the inequity in the allocation of national resources between the western, more remote areas and the eastern, more prosperous sections of the country (Liao, 2013). Hence, in 2009, the Chinese Ministry of Education and Ministry of Finance jointly initiated the Guo Pei as a step toward rectifying the situation. The rhetoric describing and justifying the teaching training program is headlined by phrases such as "satisfying urgent needs" and "promoting educational reform" (Ministry of Education, 2011). At its most basic, Guo Pei targets the development of a core set of teachers known as "seed teachers" (种子教师, zhongzhi jiaoshi) who then return to their rural provinces, districts, hometowns, and villages to teach students or to train their fellow teachers there. Substantive financial resources have been allocated into the Guo Pei, resulting in the involvement of a large number of teachers. In 2010, 550 million RMB (approximately U.S. $83 million) was invested into the implementation of the Guo Pei, involving 1.15 million teachers of which 1.1 million teachers (95.6%) were from rural and ethnically areas such as Chong Qing and Ningxia (Ministry of Education, 2011).

A multitude of programs have emerged from the generously funded Guo Pei initiative. Two national programs from the Guo Pei that demonstrate its focus on developing teacher experts and teacher trainers in the rural areas include the "Primary and Secondary Teachers' Modeling Training Program" (中小学教师示范性培训项目) and the "Mid-Western Backbone Teachers' Training Program" (中西部骨干教师培训项目) (Ministry of Education, 2012). From these main programs, Chen (2009) reports the emergence of the following diverse subprograms, namely, the Excellent Teacher Training Program for Primary and Secondary Schools in the Middle and Western Areas; Excellent Teacher Training Program for Primary and Secondary Schools in Border and Minority Areas; Teacher Trainer Training Programs; Distance Training Programs for Compulsory Education Teachers in Rural Areas in Middle and Western China; Distance Training Programs for Teachers in Curriculum Reform Experimental Areas; Training Programs for Teachers in Earthquake Areas; Training Programs for Physical Education and Art Teachers in Primary and Secondary Levels; and Knowledge and Practice for China-Training Programs for Headmasters at the Primary and Secondary Levels.

We follow this Guo Pei overview with a more detailed analysis of the foundations underlying the programs in the following section. In doing so, the achievements and challenges of the program can be better understood.

Guo Pei Approaches

Three main approaches are undertaken in programs under the Guo Pei Plan. The first utilizes theoretical or conceptual models that are developed and then applied across programs. The second is a field-based approach "teacher replacement" programs (see also Pei and Jin's Chapter 2) in which undergraduates from universities in urban centers temporarily exchange places with in-service teachers in rural areas. Finally, the third is a blended (face-to-face and online) approach to providing instruction.

Theoretical Model Application

A perusal of Guo Pei literature in China (e.g., Shi, Yang & Zhu, 2011; Yu, Mei & Wang, 2011; Li & Wang, 2012; Wang & Cai, 2013) brings forth the fact that there is heavy reliance on theoretical models that are developed and applied in various Guo Pei programs. We provide here four examples of models that are most often used and perhaps most well-known.

Wang and Cai (2013) developed the "knowledge-capability-practice-experience" (KCPE) model for the Mid-Western Backbone Teachers' Training Program. Wang and Cai claim that the model is based on David Ausubel's 1968 meaningful learning theory as well as other theories of teaching and developmental learning. True to one of Ausubel's principles of learning, the thrust of the model is uncovering what rural teachers and administrators already know about, namely, what they see as urgent needs and problems in what they are doing and in the place where they are doing it. By going through what Wang and Cai identify as the problem-identification stage with these central stakeholders, specific issues and gaps in their knowledge can be organically identified and targeted. The teachers and administrators are then to apply knowledge they receive, and they are supported in this endeavor by observations and appraisals by experts in the field. The model, it is argued, enables Guo Pei–based programs that use it to be more relevant and contextualized. We translated the model from its original source in Figure 7.1.

The next model in use is the "Four-Stage Model" created by Li and Wang (2012) and is used in Chong Qing in the Excellent Teacher Training Program for Primary and Secondary Schools in the Middle and Western Areas. Although theoretical learning continues to be the foundation for the model as in the Wang and Cai (2013) model, that stage is accompanied by teachers shadowing the practice of experts and reflecting jointly with a panel of experts and peers before proceeding to implement what they have learned. In the model, this shadowing is part of the "Training and Implementation" stage (see Figure 7.2). In that stage, the shadowing follows "pre-training" where teachers are exposed to theoretical learning. The teachers then reflect on what they observed with a panel of experts who later undertake follow-ups by observing teachers and reflecting with them jointly on their teaching and where it could be improved. It is argued thus that this model enables teachers returning to the classroom to be more informed and prepared.

Yu et al. (2011) developed a model for the Primary Backbone Headmaster Training program. They stated that teacher learning is "context learning based

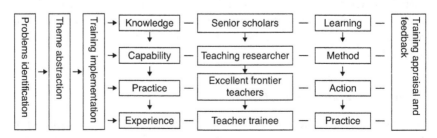

FIGURE 7.1 KCPE Teacher Training Model (Wang & Cai, 2013, p. 118)

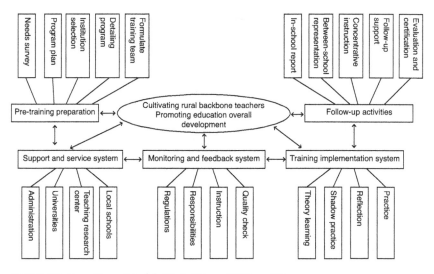

FIGURE 7.2 Four-Stage Model (Li & Wang, 2012, p. 73)

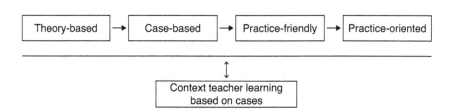

FIGURE 7.3 Contextualized Case-Based Teacher Learning

on cases" (p.180). Therefore, they organized teacher training around cases or incidences that teachers bring to the discussion table. These are discussed in terms of their interconnections with theory and how what is learned from the cases can be made appropriate and adaptable to practice. The training that follows this model goes through four stages, identified as "theory-based, case-based, practice-friendly, and practice-oriented" stages (see Figure 7.3). Because researchers and teachers are constantly in dialogues, proponents of this model argue that one of its strengths is the sense of community and collegial cooperation that develops between all involved if the model is used in the spirit intended.

Based on Shulman's (1987) "Pedagogical Content Knowledge" (PCK) concept, Shi et al. (2011) reported the use of their model (see Figure 7.4) in the Guo Pei Kindergarten Backbone Teacher Training program. In identifying with Shulman's conceptualization, developers of this model believe that teacher expertise is a combination of their subject matter and pedagogical knowledge of the context in which they teach. Thus, it is important that all teacher training and professional development should be undertaken in the place where instruction

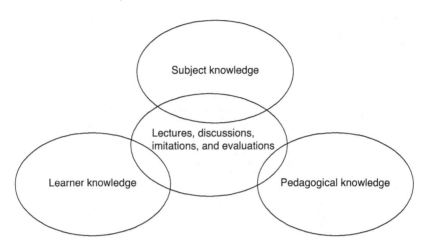

FIGURE 7.4 On-Site Classroom Training Model

happens so that all the specific circumstances that surround it could be understood and incorporated. They termed the model the "On-site classroom training model" (p. 241). Teachers' classrooms are the site and the platform for the training in which experienced teachers and/or teacher trainers observe teacher trainees undertake instruction of their subject matter in the classroom. The former (experienced teachers/trainers) then engage the latter (trainees) in pedagogical discussions about teaching the subject in question as well as provide demonstrations for the trainees who are expected to adopt and imitate the practices they observed. According to Shi et al., in undertaking this training model, teacher trainees can see how their experienced mentors link theory and practice in their specific context. This model has similarities to the jiaoyanzu model discussed in Pawan and Fan's Chapter 5. The model is translated in Figure 7.4.

The four theoretical frameworks that underlie several existing Guo Pei programs continue to evolve and change according to resources and circumstances. Nevertheless, the models do illustrate efforts to increase the relevancy of the programs through making them more contextualized and grounded in teachers' realities.

Teacher Replacement

There are two types of "teacher replacement" Guo Pei programs that use the teacher replacement field-based approach. The programs are mutually beneficial to university undergraduates and in-service teachers as both groups stand to benefit professionally from them. The former are volunteers from universities in urban centers who temporarily take over classroom teaching from in-service teachers in rural areas, so that the latter have time to pursue professional development in institutions in urban centers (Wang & Feng, 2015, p. 91). The programs are undertaken as part of a larger initiative known as the "Mid-Western Backbone

Teacher Training Program" in areas such as Henan, Xinjiang, and Guizhou provinces, that is, the western, remote parts of China.

The first program using the approach is the "shixi zhijiao/dinggang zhihuan" (实习支教/顶岗置换). One of the participating universities is Yunnan Normal University (YNU) which, in the 2016 academic year, selected 110 undergraduate volunteers to teach in middle schools in Tengchong County, a remote area in Yunnan Province. The teachers from the county were then able to attend YNU's professional development classes (J. Qi, personal communication, September 16, 2016). On the part of the undergraduates, those who performed well in their temporary teaching assignments may be recruited and may have a job as permanent teachers waiting for them in those schools when they graduate.

Another program is the "Triangle Replacement" Program (Wang & Ren, 2014). It is similar in concept to the program previously described except that undergraduate students and experienced teachers have the opportunity to teach in tandem for part of the "replacement" experience. In the partnership between Jiaying University in Guandong Province and schools in remote counties in Meizhou, an area once predominantly settled by the ethnic Hakka group, 450 undergraduates who were English majors were assigned to the 159 secondary schools for eight weeks. Four to six of them were sent to the same school to work with in-service English teachers in groups of two to three undergraduates per teacher. In this experience, the scope of benefits is expanded. The undergraduates see firsthand and become well informed about the opportunities and challenges of teaching in the rural areas as they are linked up with exemplary teachers who are experienced and most knowledgeable about teaching in such a context. The in-service teacher mentors are rewarded not only by being given opportunities to pursue teacher training programs in universities, but the experience counts as well toward their mentorship service that is necessary for honors and promotion (see Fan's Chapter 4). Finally, students in participating schools benefit from classroom instruction that combines the expertise of seasoned teachers and the new energy and ideas of novice teachers. Hence, this arrangement is seen as constituting a complete triangle of benefits.

In both versions of the "teacher replacement" programs, the participation of teacher training institutions and universities is critical. They remain invested in sending their undergraduates as teacher substitutes despite challenges discussed in the next section, particularly when they consider the benefits to learning.

The institutions and universities are a critical piece in the government's Guo Pei Plan. They provide experts who lecture, share, and discuss new educational theories and methods in sessions attended by in-service teachers who are given leave from their schools. The training sessions could be extensive. For example, the Guo Pei Program at Taiyuan Normal University involves 214 training hours with 36 periods of education theory, 60 periods of teaching practice, 112 periods of English courses, and 6 periods of educational technologies.

The "teacher replacement" program is indeed a uniquely Chinese professional development program for teachers. The last program described next, however, is a type of professional development program that is increasing in intensity globally.

Distance Education Programs

The huge resource gap between urban and rural areas has demanded the rethinking of ways and means to address educational equity on the part of the Chinese government. McQuaide (2009) reports that distance education has been accepted in China as an alternative strategy for the purpose. This is demonstrated by an official document entitled "Decision on Further Strengthening Rural Education" issued by the State Council in 2003, which stated that the medium is to be used to facilitate exchanges between urban and rural areas as a means to improve education. Following the decision, the Distance Education Project for Rural Schools (DEPRS) was launched and training and development of rural teachers became its core.

Universities such as Peking and Tsinghua universities undertake collaborations within and across agencies to bring DEPRS into fruition. Tsinghua University's efforts is a case in point. Starting from 2015, Tsinghua University's Primary School collaborated with its Poverty Relief Office in the School of Continuing Education to record and broadcast sixty English lessons taught by Tsinghua Schools teachers to 8,734 primary teachers in remote areas. Tsinghua University also has established "sister school" relationships between its elementary schools and schools in rural and ethnically diverse regions which are maintained online. Videotaped instruction of Tsinghua teachers in their classrooms are made available online for the perusal of teachers in their sister schools. These sister schools include Wuqiang County Guo Zhuang Primary School in Hebei Province; Tongyu County No. 2 Experimental Primary School in Bai Cheng City, Jilin Province; Xintian County Long Quan No. 1 Primary School in Hunan Province; and Zhengfeng County Ping Jie Central Primary School in Guizhou Province.

The university also collaborates with international and local non-governmental organizations (NGOs) in using distance education as a means to support secondary and elementary education in rural China. For example, the Hong Kong (HK) Sales Education Fund has provided support to Tsinghua to develop and implement an online training program and the establishment of "Distance Teaching Stations." The stations in various locations in remote areas of the country are used for recruiting and supporting teachers as well as providing space for them to take lessons online. The stations also organize training and test sessions for the teachers, the completion of which result in certificates issued to teachers. With the experience of over thirteen years of practice, Tsinghua University alone has been able to set up 3,600 distance education stations.

The online teacher training and professional development provided at the stations are undertaken in combination with onsite efforts. The top thirty teachers in the distance program from each online training session are invited to have a one-week face-to-face teacher training either in one of Tsinghua University's affiliated schools or in an institution in Hong Kong. At the same time, funded by the Tseng Hin Pei Charity Fund, each June, professors and young teachers of English from Tsinghua University travel to remote areas of the country to give lectures to teachers on various topics. For example, in 2008, at the Suyu County Station in Jiangsu Province, Professor Fang Yang's lecture topics were "Interpreting the curriculum criteria for elementary and middle school English teaching," "The basic methods of teaching English," and "The necessary qualities to be a teacher"; in 2009 at the Xintian Country Station, in Hunan Province, Professor Honghua He's topics covered "English teaching methodology in elementary and middle schools"; and in 2014 at the Zhongshan City Station in Guizhou Province, Professor Wenfang Fan's topics included the "IRF three-move model and communicative classroom teaching" and "Using natural phonics to teach English spelling." The lectures and demonstrations are digitally archived for use and for reference by teachers in the program.

Thus far, the program has involved 865 Tsinghua University students, 309 teachers from Tsinghua schools, 857 students from the U.S., the UK, Hong Kong, and Macao who volunteer through Tsinghua University to teach as well as demonstrate English language teaching for two weeks in the summer in the rural, western part of China (W. Fan, personal communication, September 20, 2016). As they serve teachers in 551 rural and remote counties, the Tsinghua University distance program and others like it provide an indication of the potential that exists for the online medium to be effective in providing training and professional development to teachers in the far reaches of China.

Positions on the Guo Pei Approaches

Critical positions on governmental programs such as the Guo Pei are few and far between. However, those that do exist point to the disjuncture between the theories that experts expose teachers to and their relevancy to the teachers' immediate needs in the rural areas. This is because the designers of the theoretical models in Guo Pei programs are researchers from universities or experts from training centers in urban areas. This is the case even though the Ministry of Education (MOE) stressed that those leading Guo Pei programs should be university experts familiar with best practices relevant to remote and rural areas and that two-thirds of the training experts should be from the provinces in which the programs are undertaken. As will be discussed in greater detail in Wang's

Chapter 8, because the theories and the people who put them together are removed from teachers' lives and experiences, instead of being engaged and involved, the teachers who are being trained become bystanders with minimal interest and investment in the training and professional development opportunity offered to them through the Guo Pei.

The situation is causing immediate and deep consternation in two other critical respects as well. Because the designers of these theories and teacher trainers are outsiders, the focus of the training of rural teachers has been seen as attempts toward imposing upon and altering teachers' identities (Sun, 2013, p. 42). What is meant by this statement is that the designers and trainers are seen as inadvertently molding rural teachers into thinking about themselves in ways that are more aligned to what outsiders think and do. The effort is highly undesirable to say the least and certainly not achievable in a short period of time. Furthermore, because the designers and trainers are not permanent colleagues, they have a transient and limited impact on the teachers they train. The latter will revert back to ways they know once the outsiders leave.

The situation is worsened in instances whereby the Guo Pei designers are not even English language experts but those who are from other fields who have been assigned as de facto experts in teacher training. Perhaps this is why the lecture mode, a defining and highly criticized feature of Guo Pei programs, is often resorted to, especially in instruction via distance, not only because it is familiar traditionally but also perhaps because it is the easiest way for non-experts to deliver information.

The purpose of Guo Pei is to set a model of teacher training and to develop a cadre of well-trained "zhongzi" or seed teachers. Highly qualified teachers are sent away to pursue training and professional development in the programs. In their replacement are undergraduates who serve as student teachers or temporary staff. This practice, particularly in the "dinggang zhihuan" (顶岗置换) or teacher replacement model, is considered highly problematic in several respects. First, the undergraduates' teaching readiness and classroom management ability are questioned, mainly because they are unprepared and are generally unsupervised as their mentors are often, if not always, away. Second, because these individuals are not licensed to teach, there are questions about the legality of them even being in the classroom. And third, because the undergraduate student teachers are assigned to remote locations, parents and the students themselves, especially female students, worry about their safety (see Wang & Ren, 2014).

When well-trained and highly experienced teachers leave to take part in Guo Pei programs, their schools and communities often lose their best and brightest to the programs. When this happens, the overwhelming worry of school and local officials is that such an arrangement adversely affects student performance in examinations in the long run. It is thus not surprising that Zhang and Wang

(2012) point to the lack of support from local educational authorities or schools for the programs, as well intentioned as they may be. For example, there are informally reported instances whereby officials do not send their most experienced and talented Backbone Teachers to take part in the Guo Pei programs; or that they do not send teachers who are teaching critical subjects; or that the officials do not consider it an issue when they find out that there are teachers who immediately return back to their schools right after they register for Guo Pei training so that they could meet their obligations at home (see Han & Wang, 2011). The presence of these practices suggests that there is a lack of support by officials in rural areas who may feel that the Guo Pei programs could worsen an already challenging situation in rural schools where students generally perform below the national average.

Be that as it may, Guo Pei programs have been praised in two main ways. First, the Guo Pei program, particularly the student-teacher exchange program, is considered to be an effective solution to the "learning and work" (Sun, 2013, p. 41) gap whereby what undergraduate student teachers learn in school is often not directly relevant in the workplace. By immersing the students in working in remote rural schools, they can immediately understand both the challenges and the unique opportunities that exist in teaching in such a context. In research by Wu (2012) of undergraduate student teachers in a Guo Pei–sponsored program in rural Guangxi, 88 percent of them reported an expansion of such knowledge. The undergraduates also gained in other ways evident by the fact that 94 percent of them declared an increase in their English skills and 92 percent, a better understanding of classroom management.

Second, Guo Pei programs are praised for being instrumental in helping to upgrade the quality of teachers and in addressing teacher shortage in the rural areas. The programs have increased access to training to rural teachers, 66.50 percent of whom would not have had access to any (Zhang & Wang, 2012) had they not participated in the programs. Guo Pei programs have enabled these teachers to expand their horizons, especially those who were able to leave their rural schools for big cities to obtain teacher training. Be that as it may, there is still much to be done and should be considered for the Guo Pei programs to reach their full potential.

Considerations for the Next Steps in Guo Pei Programs

Guo Pei programs are a significant experiment in which the Chinese government has invested heavily. We believe that for it to be successful the collaboration between various organizations and agencies is needed as well as openness to various approaches as the need is urgent and the undertaking is huge. Such efforts are discussed in Wang's Chapter 8. A greater increase in the partnerships between rural schools and universities in the Guo Pei programs is also needed.

At this point, the collaboration is limited to only about three comprehensive universities (Peking University, Tsinghua University, and Guangzhou University) and seven normal universities (Beijing Normal University, East China Normal University, Jiangsu Normal University, Central China Normal University, South China Normal University, Shaanxi Normal University, and Jiangxi Normal University) (Leng, Zhu & Shen, 2015, p. 67).

Collaborations with international agencies should also be increased and enhanced in Guo Pei programs. A case in point is the UNESCO Children's Fund Program in which the international agency collaborated with national-, provincial-, and district-level agencies. Not only are up-to-date teaching materials as well as equipment for music and physical education classes distributed to schools through this program, but new ideas are introduced such as the use multi-modal approaches with young polyglot indigenous children learning English (Pei & Jiang, 2016).

Programmatically, as is clear from the preceding discussions, top-down Guo Pei programs are challenging. Nevertheless, a top-down/bottom-up approach could be attempted with the rural teachers themselves as resources and co-developers of Guo Pei programs. We see the attempts already being made such as in the case-based model previously described. This is because the model is capitalizing on teacher reflectivity, which Pawan (2016, p. 15) asserts is valuable as "teacher insider" knowledge or what teachers already know can be brought to the fore in their professional development. This can increase teachers' sense of value in their expertise, the relevancy of information, and can provide a means to bridge their practice to information from outside experts. Reflective teaching models such as those by Zeichner (1984), Calderhead (1989), and Korthagen and Kessels (1999) can be starting points that guide the practice of Guo Pei programs for these reasons, particularly because they lead to increased teacher motivation and sense of investment in pursuing training and professional development.

As can be seen in our comments and in the next chapter by Ge Wang (Chapter 8), Guo Pei programs need to focus on cultural responsiveness most of all. Liao (2013) argued that such responsiveness that can only be derived from a well-developed cross-cultural competency is very important for rural English teachers. It helps teachers to not only teach students in ways that are relevant to their needs and dispositions but also to develop within them a sense of compassion and understanding so that they can make meaningful connections with their students. Thus, Yu and Tang (2012) argue that the "enhancement of teachers' cultural competence should come to the core" of rural English teacher training, which at this point is a "deficit in teachers' capability" (p. 75).

Many other suggestions exist to improve Guo Pei programs. Our chapter is one contribution toward continuing the conversation along these lines.

References

Calderhead, J. (1989). Reflective teaching and teacher education. *Teaching and Teacher Education*, *5*(1), 43–51.

Chen, X. Y. (2009). Remarks on the opening ceremony of "Guopei-Teacher Trainer Training Programs." *The Inservice Education and Training of School Teachers*, *29*(10), 3.

Han, S. L., & Wang, Zh. R. (2011). Responsibility is heavier than Tai-A critical reflection on the recommendation of teacher. *The Inservice Education and Training of School Teachers*, *9*, 5–6.

Korthagen, F. A., & Kessels, J. P. (1999). Linking theory and practice: Changing the pedagogy of teacher education. *Educational Researcher*, *28*(4), 4–17.

Leng, J., Zhu, L. L., & Shen, X. D. (2015). Distance training model featuring learning support: The case of national teacher training program in Pecking University. *Distance Education in China*, *11*, 67–71.

Li, M., Wu, Y. H., & Xu, H. M. (2006). IBM reshaped education: Teacher training model oriented to basic education in China. *E-Education Research*, *4*, 70–75.

Li, Y. T., & Wang, Zh. Q. (2012). Design and implementation of "Four Stage Model" in teaching training—taking Guopei as a case. *Journal of the Chinese Society of Education*, *1*, 71–75.

Li, Zh. Q. (2010). A research on English teacher training in the rural area. *Modern Education Science*, *2*, 108–110.

Liao, P. Q. (2013). A reflection of rural English teachers' cross culture training in "Guo Pei." *Teaching and Management*, *550*(9), 45–47.

McQuaide, S. (2009). Making education equitable in rural China through distance learning. *The International Review of Research in Open and Distributed Learning*, *10*(1), 21.

Ministry of Education. (2011). *Remarkable progress was achieved in Guo Pei*. Retrieved from www.moe.edu.cn/publicfiles/business/htmlfiles/moe/s4645/201105/120285.html

Ministry of Education. (2012). *Guo Pei Plan*. Retrieved from www.moe.gov.cn/publicfiles/business/htmlfiles/moe/s6811/201209/141516.html

National Bureau of Statistics, P.R.C. (2011). *The communique of Sixth national population census*. Retrieved from www.stats.gov.cn/tjsj/tjgb/rkpcgb/qgrkpcgb/201104/t20110428_30327.html

Pawan, F. (2016). Reflective pedagogy in online teaching. In F. Pawan, K. Wiechart, A. Warren & J. Park (Eds.), *Pedagogy and practice in online language teacher education*. Alexandria, MD: TESOL Press.

Pei, M., & Jiang, Q. (2016). Flourish of TPR in minority schools in Teng Chong, Yunnan. *Teachers' Journal*, *3*, 44–48.

Shi, Y., Yang, J. C., & Zhu, L. (2011). On-site classroom training model. In National Teacher Education Curriculum Committee (Ed.), *A complete of cases in Guo Pei program*. Beijing: Higher Education Press.

Shulman, L. (1987). Knowledge and teaching: Foundations of the new reform. *Harvard Educational Review*, *57*(1), 1–22.

Sun, Y. (2013). Historical transcendence and realistic barrier in the "National Training Plan." *Theories and Practice of Education*, *33*(22), 41–44.

Wang, B. S., & Feng, Y. H. (2015). Difficulties and solutions in implementation of "Guo Pei Plan." *China Educational Journal*, *10*, 88–92.

Wang, B. S., & Ren, Q. H. (2014). Modification and innovation of Guo Pei training patterns. *Journal of the Chinese Society of Education*, *9*, 91–93.

Wang, D. F., & Cai, Q. Y. (2013). Pattern construction of "Knowledge-Capability-Practice-Experience" in the teacher training of "National Training Project." *Curriculum, Teaching Material, and Method, 33*(7), 116–120.

Wu, H. Z. (2012). Rural middle and primary school teacher training in Guo Pei programs in the western part of China. *Journal of Teaching and Management, 6,* 56–57.

Yu, J., & Tang, Z. (2012). An exploration of training model in Guo Pei program in the perspective of competence enhancement. *China University Teaching, 5,* 74–76.

Yu, W., Mei, X. J., & Wang, J. (2011). Promoting primary headmasters' professional development through organizing teacher training facing practice and based on learning theory. In National Teacher Education Curriculum Committee (Ed.), *A complete overview of cases in Guo Pei program*. Beijing: Higher Education Press.

Zeichner, M. K. (1984). Preparing reflective teachers: An overview of instructional strategies which have been employed in pre-service teacher education. *International Journal of Educational Research, 11*(5), 565–575.

Zhang, Er. Q., & Wang, X. H. (2012). The main problems and analysis existing in teacher training—taking "National Level Teacher Training Plan" as an example. *Journal of Educational Science of Hunan Normal University, 11*(4), 36–39.

8

ENGLISH TEACHER DEVELOPMENT IN RURAL AND ETHNICALLY DIVERSE AREAS

Sowers Action Seeding the Fields

Ge Wang

Introduction

The last thirty years have witnessed the rise of China as a global power. More and more importance is placed on education as a means to build an intellectual engine for the purposes of nation building and global competitiveness. Toward that end significant resources have been allocated to the sector and comprehensive policies have been put into place, including English language policies. As mentioned in earlier chapters, since 2000, English has become a mandatory subject in the curriculum throughout the Chinese educational system from elementary to tertiary education. Despite these efforts, the quality of English teachers in ethnically diverse and rural areas of China remains challenging and problematic, necessitating the involvement of agencies at multiple levels to find ways to improve it. This chapter will highlight the efforts by a non-governmental agency, the Sowers Action (SA) (苗圃行动, Miapu Xingdong), a Hong Kong–based non-religious, non-political, and non-profit registered charity, to assist English teachers in one of the most ethnically diverse areas of southwestern China.

The Obstacles on the Ground

Resources and policies provide opportunities to improve the situation but they also exacerbate and present new problems. The former (resources) is plagued by the imbalance in its distribution and in the latter (policies), the ever-widening gap that they create in English language teaching between teachers in the coastal, urban, and metropolitan cities in the east and those in the inland, frontier, mountainous, rural, and ethnically diverse areas in the west.

The resource imbalance can be seen from the example in Table 8.1 showing the disparity in the financial allocation to students in two locations in

TABLE 8.1 2013 Per Student Budget in Public Schools (Ministry of Education, 2014)

School level	Elementary	Junior High/Middle	High School
National allocation	RMB 6,901.77	RMB 9,258.37	RMB 8,848.14
Beijing (city-level allocation)	RMB 21,727.88	RMB 32,544.37	RMB 36,763.03
Yunnan (province-level allocation)	RMB 4,979.84	RMB 7,189.98	RMB 6,802.99

comparison to the allocation at the overall national level. The imbalance adversely impacts, consequently, the extent to which teachers can be employed to teach and support them.

As can be seen, in 2013, for each elementary, junior high (middle), and high school student in Beijing, the average educational budget was RMB 21,727.88 (U.S. $3,427.11), RMB 32,544.37 (U.S. $5,133.18), and RMB 36,763.03 (U.S. $5,798.59), respectively. In contrast, students in Yunnan Province where fifty-two out of the fifty-six ethnic groups reside, the per student allocation was just RMB 4,979.84 (approximately U.S. $724.62), RMB 7,189.98 (approximately U.S. $1,046.23), and RMB 6,802.99 (approximately U.S. $989.91) for each elementary, middle, and high school student, respectively. Thus, on the whole, the fiscal allocation per student in Yunnan is about three to four times lower than that for students in big cities like Beijing and Shanghai and it is even below the national average. These imbalances consequently impact schools' ability, particularly those in the under-funded areas, to provide sufficient opportunities for training and professional development for their teachers (Guo, 2013; Hu, 2015).

It is thus not surprising that rural English teachers (RETs) in ethnically diverse provinces such as Yunnan Province have reported that the lack of such opportunities has resulted in problems such as their low sense of professional achievement and low teaching confidence (Li, 2012). RETs' frustration with the scarcity of opportunities for them to enhance and improve their knowledge and abilities is compounded with their spectacularly low remuneration system that leaves the teachers working and living in impoverished environments. This is particularly the case of temporary English teachers (代课老师, daike laoshi), who are recruited by rural villages and townships because of the severe shortage teachers in their areas. Chung and Mason's (2012) ethnographic study of life in a rural village in Yunnan Province showed that the monthly income of such a teacher is about 500 yuan (U.S. $75 approximately), which is just one third of the salary of a regular teacher, which is about 1,500 yuan (U.S. $225 approximately). Such a salary does not cover the cost of living even in the rural areas where rents could be 1,000 yuan (U.S. $150) for a one-bedroom apartment.

When it comes to policies, China has undergone three rounds of English curriculum reform over the past thirty-eight years. The first curriculum reform was called "The Primary and Secondary English Syllabus for Ten-Year Full-Time Schools," issued in 1978 by the Chinese Ministry of Education (MOE), which set the starting levels and developmental stages of English in Chinese public schools. This syllabus was revised in 1986. The second curriculum was the 2001 "National English Curriculum Standards," which called for the delineation of categories to develop students' overall ability in the language, consisting mainly of language skills, language knowledge, culture, affective knowledge, and learning strategies (Wang, 2007). The very recent English curricular reform stresses the development of English language competencies of thinking and learning in the language. According to Cheng and Zhao (2016), the reform focuses on the following:

- English language competence (language knowledge on pronunciation, vocabulary, grammar, discourse and pragmatics as well as in comprehension and engagement in English discourse);
- Cultural character development (comprehension and interpretation of cultural heritage, socio-cultural contexts as well as the ability to take and express positions on issues of culture and identity);
- Cognitive competence (comprehension of the connotation and denotation of English discourse, ability to make connections to the world at large, to develop new conceptions and to solve problems from multiple perspectives using English as a medium); and
- Learning ability (knowledge and positive motivation to use multiple methods and strategies for learning).

As is evident, the reform calls for a complex set of skills for teachers of English to develop in their learners. For RETs, their main complaint is not against the need for the skills but that the policy requiring them was developed without keeping in mind minority students in remote areas who have different schooling starting points than that of their mainstream counterparts (predominantly the Han living in large and well-resourced metropolitan areas). For example, before the rural English teachers (RETs) can address the reform requirements, they have to help ethnically diverse students who arrive at school with their own mother tongue or first language (L1) to overcome the challenge of learning English as a third language, in addition to learning Mandarin as a second language. RETs in these areas also have the monumental challenge of incorporating in their classrooms materials which are developed elsewhere in big cities and thus culturally distanced from their students' backgrounds. There is also the situation of a severe shortage of qualified teachers who speak their students' first languages (LI) to help RETs and the students they teach to navigate through the frustrations and confusion of multilingual and cross-cultural communication in classroom instruction and beyond (Yang, 2003; Yang & Song, 2006; Hu, 2007; Jiang, Liu, Quan & Ma, 2007).

The Chinese government has undoubtedly taken measures to address the problems. As discussed in detail in Pei and Jin's Chapter 7, in 2010 the Ministry of Education (MOE, 2010), together with the Ministry of Finance, launched a national teacher training program called Guo Pei Plan (国培计划) that has the main purpose of enhancing the overall quality of rural teachers in China in ethnically diverse areas of the country. The program includes the Project of Exemplary Teachers Training (PETT) as well as the Project of Rural Key Teacher Training (PRKTT) in central and western China.

A series of other measures has also been undertaken including the implementation of the Outline of Mid- and Long-Term National Educational Reform and Plan (2010–2020). It involves local governments in specifically targeting the support for elementary and secondary teachers as well as their students in the affected areas. For instance, the Outline of Mid- and Long-Term National Educational Reform and Plan of Yunnan Province (2010–2020) includes a development mechanism to unify efforts to improve education in the central and western areas of the province. Priority is placed on equity in the deployment of resources to all teachers, including equitable salary and welfare benefits, and on strengthening the teaching of their subject areas, including the teaching of English. The projects from the plan also target support for specific minority students in poverty-stricken areas, such as the dedicated assistance for Tibetan students who live in Yunnan Province, school construction and infrastructure enhancement for students who live along areas bordering Myanmar, Laos, and Vietnam. In addition, the plan also calls for projects that establish bilingual kindergartens taught by bilingual teachers in these areas.

The afore-mentioned projects consist of rigorous measures being undertaken by the local provincial government of Yunnan Province, which has invested 317 million yuan (U.S. $47.8 million) from 2010 to 2014 to implement teacher training and professional development programs at national and provincial levels (Yunnan Educational Committee, 2015). By extension, they also exemplify the Chinese government's efforts in improving education in the remote areas in the far reaches of the country.

A Non-Governmental Organization's Role in Teacher Development in Rural Areas: The Case of the Sowers Action (SA) Project

In the remote and frontier provinces like Yunnan, Non-Governmental Organizations (NGOs) (also known as Non-Profit Organizations (NPOs)) play critical roles. In this regard, the approach these organizations take is instrumental to their success. The NGOs work in partnership with communities directly and/or with agencies within them, to target their specific goals, and to use their specific resources. The organizations also have the flexibility to operate outside the boundaries of governmental funding that usually comes with conditions. In that regard, NGOs have been effective in fostering widespread education for various minority groups as well as in promoting education that uses the indigenous languages or mother tongues of people in those communities. For instance, there is the Teach for China (TFC) (美丽中国, Meili Zhongguo) project sponsored by the Beijing Lead Future Foundation (北京立德未来基金), a non-profit foundation, whose primary aims are to educate underserved children, to bring about educational equality, and to inspire young people to become leaders in the efforts (Teach for China, 2015). From 2008 to 2014, volunteer teachers were recruited from top universities both in China and in the United States They underwent a rigorous selection process. Those who were successful were then assigned to teach in rural schools under a two-year full-time contract to teach subjects that they majored in at their universities, particularly in the core subjects of mathematics, Chinese, and science. All native speakers of English were assigned to teach English in the schools. Since its establishment in 2008, TFC has sent over 600 volunteer teachers to 128 understaffed and under-resourced schools in Yunnan and Guangdong provinces and they have impacted over 100,000 students (Teach for China, 2015).

Another example is the Summer Institute of Linguistics, Inc. (SIL), which is an NGO committed to providing language service for communities. The East-Asian branch of SIL cooperated with the Yunnan Department of Education and the Yunnan Ethnic Affairs Commission to launch a program called the "Zero Barrier Bilingual Education Project" (ZBBEP) in two Yunnan minority-language communities, that is, amongst the Dai in Xishuangbanna Prefecture and the Bai in Dali Prefecture. ZBBEP focuses on sustaining the development of students' mother-tongue/LI and using bilingual approaches to teach students from the two minority groups as a means to improve their academic achievement. The implementation of ZBBEP has resulted in progress in sustaining bilingualism in students' listening, speaking, reading, and writing skills. Furthermore, improvement has been shown in students' learning abilities and in their participation in the bilingual education projects (Wang & Zhang, 2016).

The focus of the rest of this chapter turns to an NGO, the Sowers Action (SA) group, that has invested heavily (RMB 440 million, approximately U.S. $66 million) to support the education of minority students in rural and ethnically diverse areas of China. The group's English language training program in a school in Yunnan Province is showcased as a means to share deeper insight into a specific effort by an independent agency in this undertaking. The Sowers Action (苗圃行动, Miaopu Xingdong) group, established in 1992, is a Hong Kong–based non-religious, non-political, non-profit registered charity organization. The metaphoric meaning of "Sowers Action" is the sowing of the seeds of knowledge. In its earlier stage, SA invested heavily in providing student sponsorship, constructing schools and facilities but since the middle of 2000, it has begun to train teachers, particularly teachers of the English language as well as teachers of special and pre-school education. In the 2014–2015 academic year, SA operated five teacher training programs, sent out thirteen project working groups, and trained 762 local teachers. By the end of 2015, SA had funded over 1,280 school construction projects, subsidized over 295,000 primary and secondary students, 870 university students, and 28,000 teachers for teacher training programs. It is also currently operating a home for abandoned and impoverished children while subsidizing another school for orphans in a province.

SA's efforts in extensive philanthropic work and investment in improving education for minority students in ethnically diverse areas of China are further described in the following section in the specific context of a middle school. Areas of success and challenges highlight the necessity for their efforts to continue as well as to be further improved.

The Sower Action (SA) Teacher Development Project

The focus in this section is SA's project in a pseudonymously named school, the Blue Mountain Middle School (BMMS) in a remote mountainous region of Yunnan Province. Data from SA's Annual Reports, post-training reports, and working groups' reports were collected and analyzed. Interviews with thirteen individuals were conducted (see Table 8.2). They included SA volunteer teachers, permanent teachers, and BMMS' principal. Interviews were also conducted with staff members from a university that partnered with SA in the project, including the dean of its School of Foreign Languages and faculty members who volunteered to take part in the project.

TABLE 8.2 Interviewees (With Pseudonyms)

Interviewees	Background
Ping	Female, 10 years' experience in teaching English at BMMS, BA in English
Cui	Female, 6 years' experience in teaching English at BMMS, BA in English
Jun	Female, 21 years' experience in teaching English at BMMS, BA in English
Yan	Female, former English teacher at BMMS
Chang	Male, BMMS principal
Qi	Male, office director of BMMS
Sue	Female, SA teacher and provincial organizer of English teacher development program
Fang	Female, 20 years' teaching experience in English, an independent volunteer English teacher from Hong Kong
Gang	Male, MA in English, university lecturer teaching oral English and reading, in charge of Guo Pei Plan at the university
Rui	Female, MA in English, university Associate Professor
Wei	Female, PhD in TESOL, Associate Professor, 10 years' teaching experience
Jie	Female, Associate Professor, 20 years' teaching experience, university leader of English teacher development
Sheng	Male, 25 years' experience, professor and former university dean

A Profile of BMMS

Blue Mountain Middle School (BMMS) is a village school located in a county of Yunnan Province, in an ancient and mountainous area surrounded by four autonomous minority counties. Established in 1971, BMMS is under the jurisdiction of the regional county's Education Bureau, hosting over 800 students from several ethnic minority groups including the Wa, Yi, Lahu, and Dai groups. Most of the students come from farming households and do not return home until the end of the academic year due to inaccessible roads during bad weather months. School is probably the farthest they have ever been from home and for the few who managed to travel elsewhere, the county capital city of the region is probably as far as they could travel. On the part of the faculty, BMMS struggles with teacher quality and in providing support for its teachers who lack training and professional development.

The school's collaboration began with SA initiating the ground level work. SA later reached out to a university in the province to support the expansion of its work. SA started with the collaboration between an SA female volunteer (Fang) and an English teacher who was also the development organizer at the provincial level (Sue). The volunteer had twenty years of secondary school teaching experience in English and has advanced, tertiary degrees from a university. The local teacher developer, on the other hand, had been deeply embedded in the region for the past six years as part of its teacher development team.

In assessing teachers' needs, Sue and Fang developed four areas of teacher development to address, namely (1) enhancing the environment for English language learning; (2) using time effectively in the English classroom; (3) scaffolding English learning; and (4) increasing student exposure and accessibility to English examinations. The implementation of the areas took many forms. For example, to create a learner-friendly environment as a means to increase student interest, teachers were guided to use students' L1 when possible, materials and activities relevant to students' context, to engage learners in conversation, and to reduce translation activities to a minimum. To use time effectively in ways that balanced conversation and examination needs, they guided teachers to incorporate daily conversational practice with test practice using tests that were specifically designed by the teachers themselves so that they were more relevant and less intimidating. The SA volunteer and the local teacher developer also guided teachers to use students' L1 and multi-modal means (through the use of visuals and manipulatives) to scaffold teaching and testing.

The university participated in the collaboration by scaffolding and expanding upon the SA-initiated principles. It was represented by a team of English language teaching experts headed by a leading teacher developer who was also in charge of Guo Pei national projects for rural teachers in the area. (See Pei and Jin's Chapter 7.) They participated in and sustained classroom visits to support teachers, undertook teaching demonstrations and joint workshops to increase teachers' pedagogical knowledge and English language proficiency skills. All in all, over a period of three years, SA and the university collaborated in offering four training programs for BMMS teachers that took the shape described in general by Table 8.3.

Most of the English teacher development and training sessions were short term, and we concentrated on a one-week period. However, the repetition of these training sessions (12 times between 2010–2013) made up for their brevity. Some of these visits were also extended bi-annual visits by university faculty and students which can last seven to ten days each time.

TABLE 8.3 Sowers Action's Teacher Training Projects

Form	Contents	Purpose
Pedagogical and proficiency workshops	Planning and implementing English writing instruction Practicing skills in teaching reading, writing, and speaking (situated dialogue), vocabulary building Using educational technology	To update local teachers' English language pedagogical knowledge and proficiency skills
Simultaneous teaching demonstrations	Preparation, demonstration, and discussion of teaching showcased in public	To evaluate trainees' pedagogic competence
ELT seminars	Participating in seminars on the following topics: • English teaching methods • Problems in ELT • Function of teaching research groups • English learning–assisted games • Building English learning environment	To update local teachers' professional knowledge
Hands-on workshops on collective games	Participating in seminars on the following hands-on activities: • Pre-class warm-up games • Classroom teaching–assisted games • Game design competition (talent show) • Drama reading contest • Translation competition	To develop and maintain an English learning environment
Post-training portfolio and expertise planning	Teacher reflections on knowledge gained and development of concrete plans for curriculum reform in their schools	To further teachers' research awareness and abilities
Classroom visits	Bi-annual visits to observe the implementation of the SA principles (7–10 days at a time)	To give feedback on and to support teachers' practice

Outcomes for Rural Teachers: Have the Seeds Been Sown?

As with all projects, the outcomes of the training and professional development efforts described previously to support English teachers in China's rural areas will have to be contextualized and analyzed over the long term. Nevertheless, there is much to be learned at this point in time from several of the outcomes that have emerged from the Sowers Action project at BMMS in particular.

Gains and Opportunities

In 2013, curriculum reform based on SA's efforts was implemented at BMMS on a trial basis in Grades 7, 8, and 9. The results have been impressive in that fourteen BMMS students in comparison to eight students from the top-ranking school in the county obtained 110 points out of the 120 possible points. This made BMMS amongst the highest scorers in 2013 for that county. (At the provincial level, however, BMMS' scores were still considered low overall because the benchmark for passing examinations for these students is different than for mainstream students in the county.)

BMMS teachers also reported gains from the SA project, and the top five of which include the following:

- Understood the importance of creating an interesting English learning environment;
- Learned how to integrate the teaching material and introduce new information;
- Learned the importance of adequate pre-class preparation;
- Learned new rules and new ways to teaching language;
- Developed the ability of reflecting on their teaching.

Quotes from several of the teachers reiterate the gains:

> Before the training from SA, we managed reading material just by asking students to read through the text and then we give the Chinese version afterwards. That's it. Now we learn that students come up with their own questions and seek answers for themselves.
> *(Cui, BMMS English teacher, August 15, 2016)*

> What benefit us most from SA project is that they bring us new teaching theories and methodologies. This helps reflect on and change our traditional way of teaching in which we keep talking throughout the lesson.
> *(Ping, BMMS English teacher, August 29, 2016)*

As with all successful programs, administrator support is key. It is the same with the SA project at BMMS where the school principal provided sustained support to all teachers to attend all the workshops and training sessions they needed. The principal also took concrete measures to improve the English learning environment in BMMS by creating time in the school day for teachers to practice English dialogues with each other in addition to continuing the practice of sitting in and evaluating each other's classrooms. The incentives and the support the principal provided were a source of motivation:

> My headmaster often told us, if you want to carry out English activities, do not worry about money as he will look for it. What counts is that you can develop and implement these activities.
> *(Yan, BMMS English teacher, August 31, 2016)*

True to his word, after the completion of the SA project in his school, the principal sent seven English teachers to Beijing to further their understanding by attending the Total Immersion Program (TIP) and to the county capital to attend additional training by the Sowers Project. In 2016, an English teacher of BMMS was even sent to the University of Reading in the U.K. to explore further her profession by being a visiting scholar.

Teacher Challenges

The short-term professional development for the BMMS teachers, the follow-up visits as well as the principal's incentives were insufficient, however, to overcome persistent problems. The most significant was the disconnection between the cultural content of the materials utilized in the professional development program and the realities of the teachers and the students they teach. Ping, one of the BMMS middle school teachers, had the following to say:

> Some writing topics that we were encouraged to undertake, such as traveling and holidays, are too far away from our students' daily experience. They have never traveled before.
> *(Ping, BMMS English teacher, August 29, 2016)*

This insufficiency of the training to overcome this disconnection is reiterated by one of the teachers in the program who called for the training to include a change in what is in textbooks:

> Our children in rural areas cannot see the connection of English learning to their present life and future career. The content of textbooks should be close to their life. To solve this problem, ethnic culture should be integrated into the school curriculum. How do we do this?
> *(Jie, university teacher, August 5, 2016)*

Another challenge that remained despite the training and professional development that BMMS teachers experience is their inability to overcome the disparity between the national English language curriculum and their students' readiness:

> The English curriculum is ridiculous for it is unfair for the rural students. For example, our students are expected to write a passage of 70 words at the end of Grade 7, when many do not even know yet the 26 letters of the English alphabet. A large number of our students think it is hopeless for them to try to learn English. I feel so very upset about this.
> *(Fang, independent volunteer English teacher, September 1, 2016)*

The impossibility of the situation pushed this teacher (Fang) to teach English outside of class and to "borrow" lesson time from other subjects such as art. However, the teacher still found it difficult to meet the expectations of the demanding national curriculum and the examinations connected to it. No professional development programs, including the SA project at BMSS, have been able to provide a viable alternative.

Low English language proficiency of the teachers also remained unaltered by the professional development they experienced. (In a pre-workshop survey undertaken by SA over one third of those who applied to be in the program failed the basic English entrance examination into the program):

> My subject knowledge in English is OK but I am quite weak in spoken English. I can only speak some basic oral English. Now I am busy with teaching Junior three English so I pay more attention to the grammar knowledge points and have to ignore my own oral English language skills.
> *(Ping, BMMS English teacher, August 29, 2016)*

Such struggles resonate research by Dong (2012), Liao (2013), Fan (2014), and Xie (2016) who also report RETs' low English language proficiency and communicative competence continue to thwart professional development efforts for change. According to one of the teacher trainers, teachers' low proficiency was one of the reasons why the SA project at BMMS was unable to remove teachers' reliance on the traditional form of Grammar-Translation (GT) method where grammar knowledge is the focus of instruction. According to him if teachers "don't know much English, they can still teach English with GT approach" (Jie, university teacher, August 5, 2016).

Teacher Trainer and Institutional Challenges

Sowing the seeds of knowledge was a difficult enterprise for the teacher trainers themselves. There was never a shortage of SA or university volunteers. However, when they undertook the enterprise, there were several challenges.

First, the trainers were challenged by the nature of the institutions they represented. Because the Sowers Foundation was an NGO and the university was government affiliated, they had separate reporting channels as well as goals that did not always coincide with each other. The breakdown was most obvious, for example, in the post-workshop reporting. SA trainers did not share with university volunteers the results of surveys they conducted after each round of training workshops they jointly provided. As a result, university teachers/trainers did not have information on the strengths, weaknesses, and overall impact of the training.

Second, because the cooperation between SA and the university did not include the local government, and because the cooperation was based on loose and arbitrary terms, there were multiple problems including maintaining quality uniformity:

> At the university, we have to be responsible for ourselves and our activities. It was difficult to do this when we collaborated with the SA project at BMMS. We were supporting SA on an informal basis, and also did not have an official agreement with the local government. This posed a problem to set quality standards for the training.
>
> *(Wei, university teacher, September 5, 2016)*

Finally, as alluded in the previous quote, mother nature itself posed a problem to the trainers. Because BMMS is located in a very remote mountain area, traffic conditions are challenging particularly in July and August, the peak times when volunteers are available. Those months are defined by heavy rain and the constant risks of mudslides in that area, which is also prone to earthquakes. The university's administration was increasingly concerned for the safety of faculty volunteers who were traveling to BMMS.

> After a few years of collaborating with SA supporting BMMS teachers, our faculty gained a lot of knowledge from the experience. But it is hard for me to say "Yes" any more to requests for the collaboration. The major concern is faculty safety, and the university is fully responsible for it. It is just too dangerous for the faculty or for anyone to travel there during those months.
>
> *(Sheng, university senior administrator, July 16, 2016)*

Although there are persistent challenges and logistical issues that impact activities in the Sowers Project in collaboration with the university at BMMS, efforts continue to be undertaken to support rural teachers in the area.

Conclusion

In its latest national improvement plan, the Thirteenth Five-Year Plan released in 2016, China has placed significant importance on the urbanization of 60 percent of the country by the year 2020. This means that improving the quality of teachers in remote and ethnically diverse areas is one of the major steps toward the realization of this new national plan. It will require the coordinated efforts of governmental (including universities) and non-governmental agencies to ensure funding, quality, and safety are sustained.

Most of all, the description of the SA project at BMMS reiterates again that there should be an alternative to the one-size-fits-all approach to national English language curriculum to address the specific needs of rural English language teachers and their students.

RETs also need to be supported and provided opportunities to improve their English language skills along with that of their students. However, in doing so, consideration has to be given to teachers' knowledge of and use of students' first languages as a means to instruct students effectively, meaningfully, and humanely. As previously mentioned, the Chinese government is making efforts to train and hire teachers who are native speakers of the languages of students in the remote areas. If China is able to do this well, it will not only be an economic global leader that it already is, it will also be an exemplar to those countries who are striving to bring about equity through improving the education of their ethnic minority citizens.

Along those lines, it is clear from the SA project that teachers are calling for and are in need of training in culturally responsive instruction. There has to be a concerted effort to increase multicultural education and multicultural awareness in any teacher training program curricula. Teachers should be guided to go beyond the superficiality of merely inserting relevant cultural content, although it could start there. They need, most of all, to include instruction that is validating of student values, comprehensive and inclusive of all learning styles, transformative and emancipatory in their orientation toward educating students of diverse backgrounds (Gay, 2010). The modes and means to achieve culturally responsive instruction in China should be the thrust of teacher training programs if the country intends to be an inclusive nation that can move most, if not all, of its people forward toward prosperity, regardless of ethnicity and background.

References

Cheng, X. T., & Zhao, S. Q. (2016). On students' key competency in English as a Foreign language. *Curriculum, Teaching Material and Method, 36*(5), 79–86.

Chung, C., & Mason, M. (2012). Why do primary school students drop out in poor, rural China? *International Journal of Educational Development, 32*, 537–545.

Dong, A. H. (2012). Rational thinking on English teachers' professional development in rural middle schools. *Journal of Henan Institute of Science and Technology, 6*, 43–45.

Fan, X. Y. (2014). A SWOT analysis of elementary school English teachers in the mid rural China: The case of Zhoukou, Henan. *Education Exploration, 275*(5), 106–107.

Gay, G. (2010). *Culturally responsive teaching: Theory, research, and practice.* New York: Teachers College Press.

Guo, H. (2013). The study of professional development of rural English teachers in Shanxi Province. *Journal of Education Institute of Taiyuan University, 31*(1), 93–95.

Hu, D. Y. (2007). *Trilingual education of members from ethnic minority nationalities in Yunnan*. Kunming: Yunnan University Press.

Hu, J. (2015). Dilemma for rural English teacher professional development. *Journal of Shanxi Normal University, 42*, 213–214. (Postgraduate edition).

Jiang, Q. X., Liu, Q. G., Quan, X. H., & Ma, C. Q. (2007). EFL education in ethnic minority areas in northwest China: An investigational study in Gansu Province. In A. W. Feng (Ed.), *Bilingual education in China: Practices, policies and concepts* (pp. 240–256). Clevedon; Buffalo: Multilingual Matters.

Li, D. Y. (2012). On the professional development of the English teachers in junior high school. *Journal of Hebei Normal University (Educational Science Edition), 14*(6), 33–38.

Liao, B. Q. (2013). A reflection on the development of intercultural competence of rural English teachers. *Teaching and Management, 3*, 45–47.

Ministry of Education. (2010). *Announcement of the implementation of national teacher training programs at elementary and middle school level*. Retrieved from www.gov.cn/zwgk/2010-06/30/content_1642031.html

Ministry of Education. (2014). *Statistic report of 2013 national educational budget*. Retrieved from www.moe.edu.cn/publicfiles/business/htmlfiles/moe/s3040/201411/xxgk_178035.html

Teach for China. (2015). *Mission*. Retrieved from www.tfchina.org/en/about.aspx?nid=55&pid=56Wang, G., & Zhang, X. (2016). Internationalization and localization of bilingual education projects in Southwestern multiethnic areas: A study on Bai and Chinese bilingual education project in Jianchuan county of Dali Bai autonomous prefecture of Yunnan province. *Journal of Research on Education for Ethnic Minorities, 27*(2), 89–93.

Wang, G., & Zhang, X. (2016). Internationalization and localization of bilingual education projects in Southwestern multiethnic areas: A Study on Bai and Chinese bilingual education project in Jianchuan County of Dali Bai Autonomous Prefecture of Yunnan Province. *Journal of Research on Education for ethnic minorities, 27* (2):89–93.

Wang, Q. (2007). The national curriculum changes and their effects on English language teaching in the People's Republic of China. In J. Cummins & C. Davison (Eds.), *International handbook of English language teaching* (pp. 87–105). Boston: Springer.

Xie, J. H. (2016). Dilemma of newly recruited English teachers in rural elementary schools. *Journal of Heilongjiang College of Education, 35*(4), 36–38.

Yang, L. P. (2003). Thoughts on sharing global information and developing Zhuang and English bilingual education. *Journal of Nationalities Education Research, 14*(2), 66–70.

Yang, Q., & Song, Y. (2006). A survey of English teaching in the Bai-Han bilingual context. *Journal of Dali University, 6*(9), 70–73.

Yunnan Educational Committee. (2015). The construction of new system of rural teachers' professional development in Yunnan. *The Trends of Basic Education Reform, 23*, 3–6.

9

THE VISITING SCHOLARS PROGRAM

Adding a Flower to a Brocade

Faridah Pawan and Xin Chen

Introduction

The popular Visiting Scholars Program (VSP) supports Chinese public school teachers and university teachers for study abroad ranging from relatively brief periods of six to twenty-four months or more depending on the sponsorship they receive. The teachers are not, however, admitted as part of any formal, degree-terminal academic program.

This chapter looks into teachers' experiences in this program as well as that of their hosts. We interviewed fifteen Chinese visiting scholars who are currently in the U.S., fourteen potential scholars who are still in China, and six former scholars who have returned back to China. We also interviewed five U.S. hosts. In describing and discussing these experiences with the interviewees, several issues came to light including the importance of the program for the teachers' professional development and the program's sustainability.

The Quest for Success—The Chinese Dream

In Chinese history, scholars and educated individuals are known as "treasures" which also apply to the teachers in this program. Why would these "treasures" travel abroad when they have been successful in China? As was demonstrated in Fan's Chapter 4, being a fully-employed and permanent teacher endows individuals with multiple benefits. These benefits could include financial stability, a respected status, centrally located housing, and children's admission into the schools in which they teach. Given these benefits, why would teachers leave their jobs and families behind to become visiting scholars overseas and risk losing "guanxi" (关系) or close relationships with multiple networks of friends, colleagues, and influential individuals, and perhaps even risk losing their seniority in the professional ladder?

Several of the reasons can be seen in Pawan's interviews (see Pu & Pawan, 2014, p. 47) with Chinese English language teachers ($n = 14$) who were hoping to be visiting scholars; these included:

- Expansion of academic experience
- Enhancement of current academic skills
- Immersion in different cultures
- Cooperation with foreign scholars
- Mentorship from hosts
- Expansion of world view
- Creation of opportunities for family
- Fulfillment of a dream

The scholars who sought to pursue these goals in the U.S., Australia, UK, Canada, and Singapore were facilitated by the incentives offered by the Chinese government. Internationalization is a key feature in the government's efforts to modernize, enhance, and bring about advancement to Chinese education. Under the leadership of the current president, Xi Jinping, China has taken a pro-active stance toward development and engagement internationally as part of the realization of Xi's conceptualization of the "Chinese Dream" (中国梦), which is to redeem China's national greatness through all efforts that will increase prosperity and rejuvenate the nation. Thus, in this vision, it is no longer sufficient for the Chinese, as former Premier Deng said in the 1980s, to "observe things serenely, respond and manage things calmly, hold our ground firmly, hide our capabilities, bide our time and accomplish our objectives" (冷静观察, 沉着应对, 稳住阵脚, 韬光养晦, 有所作为). Instead, Chinese citizens are called upon to be proactive in engagement at all fronts, including internationally.

Education is perceived to be at the forefront of this strategy and is in concert with the national emphasis on international engagement. The Chinese Ministry of Education (MOE), for example, states that international exchange and cooperation are an important means to enhance the intellectual capacity and reputation of Chinese institutions (Ministry of Education of the People's Republic of China, 2004). To this end, two large-scale government initiatives are already in place; Projects 211 and 985 are complementary programs to bolster 100 Chinese institutions of higher education and to propel approximately 40 of these universities to achieve world-class status in teaching and research. In terms of Project 211, research, management, and institutional efficiency within disciplinary areas are the focus in the targeted universities. In terms of the latter (985), the aim is for the universities to reach advanced international standards in all their undertakings so as to be globally competitive. The most recent initiative is labelled as

"C9" where nine specific universities are targeted by 2020 to "be at or near world class levels" (Yang & Welch, 2012, p. 647). The universities targeted in all these three programs are amongst the highest-ranked Chinese institutions including Peking, Tsinghua, Fudan, Zhejiang, and Nanjing universities as well as Shanghai Jiao Tong, Xi'an Jiao Tong, Harbin Institute of Technology, and the University of Science and Technology of China in Anhui. Accordingly, the push to internationalize Chinese education through programs such as the Visiting Scholars Program is a key component of this initiative, defined by the pursuit of mutually beneficial strategies of engagement with all nations, including engagement with their scholars.

The university programs mentioned in this chapter impact both university teachers and public school teachers. English language teachers, along with their colleagues who teach other subject areas tested in the university entrance examinations (gaokao), have to be able to meet the challenge of preparing their students to qualify for admission into China's universities. Approximately 10 million students take the examinations annually and 75 percent of them gain admission into universities in mainland China. Though the percentage reported is high by global standards, admission into prestigious Chinese universities, however, is extremely competitive. For example, an applicant to Peking University who is from an area outside of Beijing may only have a 1 in 7,826 chance of getting in (Wong, 2012).

The Enablers for Overseas Experiences

Two main agencies associated with the Chinese Visiting Scholars Program (VSP) include a dedicated governmental agency to support university scholars as well as regional and district education offices to support teachers. The Chinese Scholarship Council (CSC) is tasked with providing financial assistance and managing the affairs of Chinese citizens studying abroad (as well as foreigners studying in China). Although most of their funds are directed to teachers at the tertiary levels, they have a robust program for public school teachers as well. This includes, for example, a special program for the "Young (under 40) Backbone Teachers" Program.

There is extensive funding allocated to the VSP, as can be seen from the numbers of individuals who will be supported as of 2016 (see Table 9.1). For many scholars, salaries continue during their time abroad and their round-trip ticket is paid for. In addition, they receive stipends of U.S. $1,400–1,800 per month, depending on the hosting institution's location, to cover their lodging and daily expenses.

The rigorous process of application is outlined in Pu and Pawan's (2014) book. The main requirements are that pre- and in-service teachers must be under forty-five years of age and have at least five years of working experience if they have a bachelor's degree. For those with a master's degree, only two years of teaching experience is required. Although teaching experience is not as important for applicants with doctoral degrees who are teaching at the university

TABLE 9.1 Chinese Visiting Scholars Programs (China Scholarship Council, 2016)

CSC Programs	Number of applications to be accepted
1. Government-funded senior scholars, visiting scholars, and post-doctoral scholars	3,500
2. Government-funded graduate study for doctoral programs	8,500
3. Government-funded graduate study for master's programs	800
4. Exchange program for outstanding undergraduates	4,200
5. Young Backbone Teachers' overseas study	3,800
6. Local government- and industry-funded senior scholars, visiting scholars, and post-doctoral scholars	2,950
7. Talent fostering for regional problems research and governmental exchange scholarships	1,950
8. Talent fostering for art	300
9. Cooperative programs with foreign countries (e.g., Fulbright)	2,500
10. Internship program in international organizations	21

level, they must be under forty years of age. In addition, applicants must receive official invitations from faculty members in overseas institutions, indicating agreement to host the applicants' visits.

For teachers at the public school level, specifically, CSC's funding is usually combined with financial support from provincial education departments, district educational bureaus, and/or funding from their own schools. There are also private agencies that support teacher groups to travel abroad such as the Bao Tian Ren Publishing House. For these teachers, there are often specific exchange programs or a set of courses pre-determined for them to engage in by the participating schools or agencies.

Complementing CSC's efforts to encourage teachers to be visiting scholars are the employment requirements of Chinese institutions. For example, in order for teachers to be promoted, particularly to a teaching position in higher institutions, overseas experiences can be obligatory. The following quotes from two visiting scholars are illustrative of the expectations:

> My school, as well as many universities, has explicitly required overseas experiences for promotion. They also prefer recruiting new faculty with overseas experiences.
>
> *(Meng, university teacher, August 21, 2016)*

> Even if I get my doctoral degree, it will be hard for me to get a job in my own university because they prefer recruiting people who graduate from better universities than us or those who have studied abroad.
>
> *(Wei, university teacher, August 29, 2016)*

For teachers in the public schools, overseas experiences and backgrounds are increasingly valued and are an asset for candidates seeking teacher positions, especially in well-resourced schools. (See Appendix 9.1 for Tsinghua High School teacher recruitment document.) For others, their school initiatives, schools' status or their own status as "backbone" or expert teachers can be (although not always) the basis for their selection to go overseas:

> There is a trend for more and more public schools to establish international divisions and teach international courses. Thus, teachers with overseas experiences will have advantages and more opportunities in public schools such as where I teach.
>
> *(Zhang, middle school teacher, August 16, 2016)*

> There are no explicit requirements for overseas experiences for public school teachers, so far, but I know schools prefer those teachers with such experiences. I think this is because schools are in great need of high quality teachers. For example, our school recruited just this year a teacher who was at New York University.
>
> *(Duan, high school teacher, September 19, 2016)*

> I was fortunately recommended by my school to apply for the program. My school is one of the top schools in our province. I was interviewed by several university professors. They mainly assessed my English proficiency. But I know several teachers in our cohort of visiting scholars who were not proficient in English but they still were selected because they are famous teachers in the province and are experts in their area.
>
> *(Cao, high school teacher, September 20, 2016)*

It is clear that overseas experiences as visiting scholars are sought-after opportunities for English language teachers at all levels. This chapter continues with a closer look at the experiences from the perspective of the scholars as well as their hosts.

Description of the Visiting Scholars Program

Requirements for ELTs as Visiting Scholars

It is common knowledge that English language teachers at the public school and university levels often obtain opportunities to go overseas. One of the reasons is that these applicants are usually the ones most capable of meeting the strict English language proficiency pre-requisite (Pu & Pawan, 2014) due to their expertise in the subject matter they teach. (See the section "Opportunities and Challenges.")

English language teachers with a bachelor's degree in English may be eligible to go to English-speaking countries without additional requirements. For others, they may have to demonstrate, for example, a score of 80 or above on the Internet version of the Test of English as a Foreign Language (TOEFL); 5.5 or above on the International English Language Testing System Examination (IELTS); or level 5 on the Chinese Ministry of Education's Public English Test System (PETS).

All Chinese visiting scholars, regardless of their levels, have to carefully outline their study plans in the application to CSC. To be competitive, the English language teachers (ELTs) have to show that research will be a central objective of their activities overseas and their learning objectives. Research is a familiar requirement for teachers at all levels—even for Chinese public school English language teachers (ELTs). Commonly, they are expected to participate in joint research with their jiaoyanzu groups (see Pawan and Fan's Chapter 5). Their participation in the research becomes part of their annual progress report and their promotional prospects are increased if the research is published. In terms of learning objectives, the main focus of the study abroad plan should be learning about culture and language teaching pedagogy.

An analysis of visiting scholar applications to a language teacher education program in a U.S. university demonstrates a wide spectrum of interests related to the research and learning objectives previously described. These fall into the following categories:

- Research methods: For example, conducting qualitative research in education such as through classroom-based approaches of action research and practitioner inquiry.
- Research on educational management and governance: For example, the use of Open Educational Resources (OER) on teacher research and participatory governance of language programs.
- Research and pedagogical training: For example, bilingual and bicultural approaches, learning styles, learner autonomy, learner engagement.

Opportunities and Challenges

The goals identified were pursued in various ways by the scholars interviewed with different outcomes and challenges.

Opportunities Created

The following quotes illustrate a combination of experiences. Although research was their target, the opportunities that presented themselves to the teachers when they arrived at their institutions led to different outcomes. These included, for one teacher, daily attendance in language classrooms to improve proficiency in the English language:

> We took classes every day from 8am to 4pm. The language teaching courses were very intensive. The program also involved language training and some social activities.
>
> *(Ma, elementary school teacher, October 29, 2016)*

Their hosts also facilitated classroom observations which the teachers noted would have been impossible to achieve without the former's help:

> I have also visited some public schools here with my host. I went to the classes that he was supervising. We sat at the back and watched the teacher teach. I also observed the teacher debriefing session that my host professor had with the teacher. . . . It was special. It is difficult to visit American classrooms on my own. I understand that the public schools have their own rules and concerns. Without my host, I would not have been able to go in.
> *(He, high school teacher, August 30, 2016)*

> My host professor made contact with several other professors. Because of it, they allowed me to attend their classes. I think they call it "auditing" classes. In one class, I read all the materials that we were assigned. The professor in the class also asked me to lead discussions on language teaching using technology in in China. I liked that.
> *(Wen, university teacher, October 29, 2016)*

Research goals were also attained particularly by teachers with well-defined research goals and by those whose research skills and interests converged with that of their hosts. Teacher Tang's quote is illustrative of the former:

> I had two goals for my U.S. visiting experience: I wanted to finish my research project with a UK university in Nottingham and also a project for my school. At the end I finished two-thirds of my research for the UK using the library resources at my host university in the U.S. I loved the library because I can get online resources from everywhere, not just from the U.S. but also from the UK and China. It was a very good chance for me.
> *(Tang, university teacher, September 9, 2016)*

For her part, teacher Xu and her faculty host found they had a common research interest which drew them together as fellow researchers and co-authors:

> I was lucky because my host was researching a topic I knew something about. I did research with her, wrote and published a paper with her. I also learnt a lot about English academic writing in the process. We revised the paper upon feedback. Even the process of revising the paper was a rewarding experience. For example, we worked together on the feedback the editors gave. By working that way, I also learnt how to respond to the editors in the process of getting the paper eventually published a year later.
> *(Xu, university teacher, October 29, 2016)*

As mentioned, all public and university teachers, as visiting scholars, are not admitted as part of any formal academic program. Public school teachers, however, may have special programs designed for them, but they remain outsiders to the institutions in which the programs exist. For university teachers, the situation can be quite different in that they are mostly responsible for structuring their own time. The success of their experiences depends on how the university teachers are able to find ways to navigate through the host's institutional systems and programs.

Challenges and Obstacles

The interviews also yielded challenges in the experiences of the teachers as visiting scholars. First and foremost, although the teachers met the pre-requisite language requirements and were functional in English, they still encountered problems:

> . . . When I was in the class, I did have something to say in the discussion but I could not fully express myself. I hope that I can in the future but I have a long way to go, I realize because I don't have that kind of training to use English.
> *(Huang, middle school teacher, April 15, 2016)*

> My English is not proficient enough. . . . I had trouble especially with writing for different contexts. The English academic writing expected in that class was especially difficult and I could not take part in it.
> *(Xie, university teacher, September 9, 2016)*

> In the library [where I spent a lot of time], I am a slow reader in English so reading English materials is quite demanding for me.
> *(Lin, university teacher, August 5, 2016)*

The problems articulated by these comments could partly be due to the teachers' lack of familiarity with the conventions and skills necessary to function in a U.S. academic environment. These are illustrated by the following teacher quotes:

> In the class I tried to take part in, I remember I got into trouble. My professor told me that my work was unacceptable as I needed to cite all the sources in my paper. I was told I was plagiarizing. I was shocked because I didn't realize that something I did was plagiarism and it was totally not intended.
> *(Sun, high school teacher, August 7, 2016)*

> There are more resources online and in the library than at home. I do need to have what they call, "information literacy" to sort out the most relevant resources. This is something to learn and it takes time which I do not have.
>
> *(Han, high school teacher, September 8, 2016)*

Other challenges that stood out by themselves were more personal in nature. Issues of identity was an example:

> My peers in the program were younger than me and I was a little confused about my identity. Most of the teachers who want to travel are younger teachers than me. I am half a teacher and half a student but most of the time, I see myself as a teacher because I have more experiences and responsibilities than a mere student. I am not sure how to present myself to the people around me and to people in my cohort.
>
> *(Xu, public school teacher, August 10, 2016)*

Having to take charge of one's own personal work habits and motivation also proved to be a challenge for this teacher:

> You don't have class that you are obliged to take and no one will tell you what you should do for your study or research. People will tend to be lazy if they don't have a set schedule. There is no peer support here and no peer pressure either. I need to set goals for myself and push myself.
>
> *(Hao, university teacher, October 19, 2016)*

Although the difficulties expressed in the foregoing quotes were similar to difficulties encountered by many other visiting scholars and newcomers to U.S. academic institutions, there were other challenges expressed that were unique to the Chinese teachers:

> We were told only when we got to our host institution, that the courses we could observe or be a part of, were those predetermined by the Education Bureau in our province. The Bureau even had set up a special program of courses for us to take. I feel that this is a restriction that are imposed on public school teachers who go overseas. We did not have freedom to choose.
>
> *(Shi, high school teacher, October 16, 2015)*

> I do not like to have to be in the Chinese community all the time here. When you go to a place where there are other Chinese, this is what happens. I came to the U.S. for a new experience, new things. It is a struggle to stay away and learn new things on my own.
>
> *(Li, middle school teacher, September 20, 2016)*

One of the problems for Chinese public school teachers is that they are not allowed to bring their family with them.

> My son was only 3 at the time I left. I missed him and worried about him a lot.
>
> *(Xiang, high school teacher, September 9, 2016)*

It needs to be mentioned here that Chinese university teachers are not always restricted from bringing along their family members and, in fact, this may be one of the incentives for these teachers to travel abroad (Pu & Pawan, 2014). However, when they do so, there are other problems that emerge, including the inability for them to focus on their academic endeavors:

> My son came with me so I could help him apply for a university. But I had much to do with him. I was very worried because I really did not have enough time for my studies.
>
> *(Feng, university teacher, October 26, 2016)*

As indicated earlier in this chapter, one of the main visiting scholar goals, particularly at the tertiary level, is collaboration with foreign experts, but this was a challenging goal to achieve and did not always happen automatically due to concerns in the incompatibility of expertise and skills:

> Actually I wanted to teach a class to demonstrate my pedagogy for K3–K6 students [third to sixth graders] but I was not allowed to. The teachers there had concerns about the pedagogy and I did not have permission. In the future, I do hope we can also get some opportunities to share and practice our teaching methods in the U.S. context.
>
> *(Feng, elementary teacher, August 9, 2016)*

> I also wanted to join a doctoral student research group led by my professor host. But I was not invited to do anything but just to listen and observe. Everybody in the group had research knowledge and skills they learned together. I did not fit in.
>
> *(Wang, university teacher, August 16, 2016)*

Despite these challenges, the Chinese teachers we interviewed unanimously indicated that interest remains high amongst their colleagues in the Visiting Scholars Program. However, there was concern about the declining number of these overseas visiting scholar opportunities over the past five years. Several reasons for this could include the inequity in the dissemination of opportunities that disadvantage teachers in rural areas, under-resourced schools, and schools not affiliated with any of the universities that are targeted in the high-profile programs such as the 985 program mentioned earlier. (See Wang's Chapter 8.) There is also the reality of China's own status as the world's second-largest economy which indicates that it is now a country with sufficient resources. There are thus fewer programs from external agencies to fund Chinese teachers and their overseas hosts (Pu & Pawan, 2014).

Be that as it may, the decline in visiting scholar opportunities could also be an outcome of the Chinese government's clamp down on corruption. Its anti-corruption rhetoric may have indirectly impacted the Visiting Scholars Programs in that they could potentially be perceived as subject to cronyism and favoritism, utilized to enhance personal benefits, or even to fund opportunities to flee overseas to escape scrutiny or prosecution (see Huang, 2016). In higher education, the issue of plagiarism has also been included in discussions of corruption. For example, several unscrupulous Chinese scholars have been accused of publishing the work of others as their own (Yang, 2005), perhaps because they have had access to resources through overseas travel made possible by their influential positions in academia.

Sustainability of Overseas Visiting Programs: A Flower Is Not Complete in Its Beauty Without Its Leaves

Sustainability of Visiting Scholars Programs can also be viewed from the perspective of the faculty hosts who are the other critical half of their Visiting Scholars Program. Chinese teachers usually identify potential hosts through their own research and individual communications with the help of recommendations on social media, colleagues, and mentors.

Because the hosts are co-participants in the programs, their views are also important for assessing the VSPs. We interviewed five U.S. university professors from a Tier 1 U.S. university who are serving in this capacity. (Tier 1 universities are research-focused universities with large endowments.) The interviewees included an assistant professor, an associate professor, a clinical professor and two full professors. For these professors, the recurring reasons for them to engage with visiting scholars include a desire to gain new insights in their discipline, broaden their scope of contacts to engage internationally, and increase the diversity of opinions and information in their classrooms. There are also China-specific reasons exemplified by the following two quotes:

> Through the experience I had with helping my Chinese scholar, I learned something new. I realized that Chinese students are firmly lodged in the product model, the pre-Flower and Hayes process writing, in the structural approach; and grammar translation approach. It is hard to overcome. I also now see that when I see a paper with 5–6 pages of extensive background information and one page of argument, I know that my Chinese students are resorting to their polite register. They do not presume that it is their role to tell readers what to think.
>
> *(John, Clinical Professor, August 20, 2016)*

Another professor sees the possibility of expanding his interests and influence in China, with the help and support of a visiting scholar he hosted in a previous year:

> The last time I gave a talk on China, my visiting scholar from last year came to attend my talk. We had a blast. She was asking good questions in the talk, made people think, connected me with other people. She and I communicate on social media all the time. . . . Every time a colleague goes to China, I send along books so that she can have them and use them to share some of the ideas in the books in China.
> *(Thomas, Professor, September 22, 2016)*

Nevertheless, there are challenges to the ability of these professors to host scholars. First and foremost, each host reported that they receive frequent and regular email requests throughout the year to host Chinese visiting scholars who are teachers. Among the five interviewed, they have hosted approximately twenty-five Chinese visiting scholars over the past five years. Given the intensive nature of these professors' research work as well as the number of students they teach and provide research supervision for, visiting scholars add substantial and sometimes unwelcome responsibilities to their already heavy workload. These factors as well as the scholars' expectations do not always match those of the professors' negatively impacts the latters' interest in hosting new visiting scholars in the future:

> There is no return in investment for me. I just make space for them in my classroom but most of the time I get nothing back. I am very busy with work here and I am considering seriously of not hosting anymore.
> *(Michael, Associate Professor, August 11, 2016)*

> I feel that my brains are being constantly picked on, and I am being constantly used for my resources. I also receive many informal requests for help sometimes not for academic help. I feel as a host I am being asked to help someone to go to college.
> *(John, Clinical Professor, August 17, 2016)*

> There is a mismatch of expectations when they arrive. Most of the time, they do not know why they are here and what they want. It is hard for me to make suggestions and they are often not on target. I also do not like to impose on my colleagues or other people to ask for favors when I myself am not clear as to how the scholars would perform in their classes or in their research group.
> *(Richard, Assistant Professor, August 18, 2016)*

> They are not as prepared as my other students in the class. They have not read everything or had the prior training. Their attendance can be

unpredictable. It can be difficult for me to include them as a full-fledged member of the class. I also cannot always include them in research either as it takes years for me to train even my own students to be ready for the research that I do.

(Susan, Professor, September 20, 2016)

As the saying at the beginning of the section states, the beauty of a flower cannot be fully realized without its leaves. Similarly, the potential and continuation of the Chinese Visiting Scholars Program, as well-intentioned and popular as it is, may be limited if it is not undertaken in the most conducive contexts with all individuals involved being able to see and reap substantive benefits from the program.

Conclusion

The chapter thus concludes with a call to the sponsors of Chinese Visiting Scholars Programs to create conditions for mutual satisfaction and benefit to be derived from the collaboration between both parties (visiting scholars and hosts). In this regard, we suggest a collaborative framework to be used as guidance for the undertaking. An example is D'Amour's (1997) Interprofessional Collaboration Framework, shown in a modified form in Table 9.2.

The first two dimensions (finalization and interiorization) of the model provide insight into collaboration via two interactional/interpersonal factors and two (governance and formalization) organizational mechanisms impacting collaboration. In terms of the first set of factors, D'Amour (1997) describes the interpersonal legwork necessary for collaborators which includes the sharing of common goals and vision and the development of a sense of mutual trust and respect for each other, particularly in each other's contributions to one another. Governance and formalization constitute structural and organizational factors which are defined by individual and/or a collective leadership particularly in explicitly articulating collaborative actions and procedures and most important, in creating conducive conditions for collaborations to take place.

The framework suggests that the sponsors should develop a well-defined infrastructure to support the collaboration they intend their scholars to have

TABLE 9.2 D'Amour's (1997) Model of Structuring Interprofessional Collaboration

Interaction Factors (in interpersonal relationships)	
Finalization	Shared Goals and Vision
Interiorization	Sense of Dependency, Mutual Trust, Respect for Mutual Knowledge
Organizational Factors (in mechanisms that regulate work)	
Governance	Central, Local, Expert Leadership
Formalization	Explicit Norms and Formalization of Structures of Collaboration

with overseas hosts. This could be in the form, for example, of engaging the teachers in well-defined preparation programs for their sojourn abroad. When these programs also involve their hosts, they give both sides chances to understand, assess, and align their interests as well as capacities. Pawan and Ortloff's (2011) research on teacher professional collaboration show that this type of preparation, especially when organizationally spearheaded by leadership, is essential. Otherwise, the collaboration will be a "hit-or-miss" experience for all involved.

APPENDIX 9.1

Recruitment Information From Tsinghua University Primary School

招聘岗位 Position	学科 Subject	名额 Quota	岗位说明 Requirements
专任教师 Teacher	语文 Chinese	3 (含分校)	1. 有一定的课堂组织能力和课程开发能力，胜任班主任工作和语文学科授课； 2. 普通话标准(二甲以上)。
专任教师 Teacher	数学 Math	2 (含分校)	1. 有一定的课堂组织能力和课程开发能力，胜任班主任工作和数学学科授课； 2. 除数学外，还具有一定科学或信息技术等课程与教学研究素养。
专任教师 Teacher	英语 English	2 (含分校)	1. 具有国际视野，口语好，口音纯正； (Must have international perspective, is proficient in oral English, and has good pronunciation) 2. 有长期留学背景优先。 (Experience in a long-term overseas study program is preferred.)
专任教师 Teacher	体育 P.E.	1 (含分校)	1. 足球、武术专业优先； 2. 具有长期体育社团指导经验。
专任教师 Teacher	学校助理 Administrative Support	1 (含分校)	1. 具有3年以上管理类工作经验； 2. 举止文雅、内涵博雅，中英文口语表达及文字写作能力强； 3. 工作责任心强、富有创新精神，组织管理能力强； 4. 执行能力强，具有抗压能力。

Source: Tsinghua University Primary School. (2016). *Tsinghua University Primary School 2016 Recruitment Information*. Available from www.qhfx.edu.cn/html/recruit

References

China Scholarship Council. (2016). 2016年国家留学基金资助出国留学人员选派简章 [General Regulation of State-funded Study Abroad 2016]. Retrieved from www.csc.edu.cn/article/280

D'Amour, D. (1997). *Structuration de la collaboration interprofessionnelle dans les services de santé de première ligne au Québec*. (Thèse de doctorat). Université de Montréal, Montréal.

Huang, C. (2016, January 13). President Xi Jinping pledges to revamp China's sweeping anti-corruption campaign. *South China Morning Post*. Retrieved from www.scmp.com/news/china/policies-politics/article/1900500/president-xi-jinping-pledges-revamp-chinas-sweeping

Ministry of Education of the People's Republic of China. (2004). 教育部 财政部关于继续实施"985工程"建设项目的意见 [Ministry of Education and Ministry of Finance comment on the continuation of the 985 project]. Retrieved from www.moe.edu.cn/srcsite/A22/s7065/200406/t20040602_174769.html

National Basic Foreign Language Teaching Research Center. (2008). 中小学优秀外语教师出国留学奖学金项目概况 [Overview of the Scholarship Program for Outstanding English Teachers in Public Schools to Study Abroad]. Retrieved from www.tefl-china.net/Article/ShowArticle.asp?ArticleID=783

Pawan, F., & Ortloff, J. H. (2011). Sustaining collaboration: English-as-a-second-language, and content-area teachers. *Teaching and Teacher Education*, 27(2), 463–471.

Pu, H., & Pawan, F. (2014). *The pedagogy and practice of Western-trained Chinese English language teachers: Foreign education, Chinese meanings*. New York: Routledge.

Wong, E. (2012, June 30). Test that can determine the course of life in China gets a closer examination. *New York Times*. Retrieved from www.nytimes.com/2012/07/01/world/asia/burden-of-chinas-college-entrance-test-sets-off-wide-debate.html

Yang, R. (2005). Corruption in China's higher education system: A malignant tumor. *International Higher Education*, 39, 18–20.

Yang, R., & Welch, A. (2012). A world-class university in China? The case of Tsinghua. *Higher Education*, 63(5), 645–666.

Yin, C. (2013). *Achievements and challenges of China's diplomacy in 2012*. China Institute of International Studies. Retrieved from www.ciis.org.cn/english/2013-06/03/content_6001789.htm

10

NEW CHINESE EDUCATION REFORM TARGETS ENGLISH

U.S. and Chinese Scholars' Perspectives

Faridah Pawan and Niya Yuan

Introduction

In October 2013, the Beijing Municipal Education Commission (BMEC) drafted a statement calling for the removal of English as one of the core subjects to be tested on the gāokǎo (high test), the National College Entrance *Examination* (NCEE). The statement, identified as the "Beijing Draft" was published in the document *Reform Framework for College Entrance Examinations and Recruitment 2014–2016*. The Draft brought about extensive discussions in the media, with members of the public expressing both support for and arguments against what the Draft was asserting. (See, for example, Zhao, 2013; Meng, 2014; Xiang, 2014; Luo, 2015.)

In the midst of the heightened public interest and scrutiny, BMEC withdrew the 2013 Beijing Draft. The Chinese government through the State Council, its main administrative branch, asserted control over the English gāokǎo reform by the release in September 2014 of the official government document, *The Implementation Opinions on Deepening the Reform of Examination and Admission System* (The Implementation Policy, 2014). As of 2016, no information on the original Beijing Draft can be found on BMEC's website.

With the Chinese government's high-level involvement, reforming English in the gaokao is now a matter of official policy. English language educators and researchers alike need to examine the consequences of the reform as, first and foremost, it impacts a significantly large number of people. In China, the examination is taken by approximately 9 million students annually in a country with approximately 440–650 million English learners (ELs) (He & Zhang, 2010). This EL population approximates or exceeds the 438 million combined populations of the "inner circle" of English-speaking countries (Higgins, 2003) of the U.S., Canada,

Britain, Australia, and New Zealand. There are approximately 1 million Chinese foreign language teachers and 180,000 expatriate teachers, most of whom are involved in English language teaching (Ministry of Education (MOE), 2003).

Finally, the English gāokǎo reform is also significant as it indicates that the status of English in China is in flux and raises issues of immediate concern in English language education within and beyond the country's borders.

Reform Description

Six years after the founding of the People's Republic of China in 1949, English was re-introduced in secondary schools where, previously, only Russian had been taught as a foreign language. In 1962, English became part of the entrance examination for colleges and universities, but the revival of English in the Chinese curriculum was temporarily suspended by the Cultural Revolution (1966–1976). Interest in English was re-ignited in China when, in 1978, Deng Xiaoping announced the Four Modernization and Open-Door Policy, at which time English language teaching resumed in earnest, and English was eventually re-instated as a compulsory subject at both secondary and tertiary levels (Liu, 2008). In 1993, a pilot reform plan called "3 + 2" model promoted English as one of the three core college-entrance examination subjects besides Mathematics and Mandarin. The remaining two can be student-selected subjects to be examined. Subsequently, the status of English in China also benefitted from heightened expectations for international engagement. These have been fueled by the country's 1998 acceptance into the World Trade Organization (WTO), its success in hosting the 2008 Olympic Games, and its status since 2010, as the world's second-largest economy with a currency (yuan) that has recently acquired the global reserve status. Nevertheless, China's national language policy now appears to be shifting again as evidenced by both the Beijing Draft and in the State Council's (Chinese central government) official position, indicating that views and policies about English in China are in flux.

The Beijing Draft urged for the removal of English from the gaokao to begin in the year 2017 and to be fully implemented by 2020. English would be assessed through two examinations separate from the gaokao that were to be available twice a year (June and January). Only the higher of the scores from one of the two examinations would be considered in students' college application. Second, the maximum score for English which counts toward university admission in China (out of a total of 750 points for all subjects) would be reduced to 100 points instead of the 150 points currently assigned to English examination results. Finally, the Draft advocated for the continuation of the practice of giving leeway to Chinese local provinces to research, develop, and administer English language examinations.

However, as mentioned in the introduction, the Beijing Draft and its contents have been withdrawn. The only document that can be referred to on the English gāokǎo reform is the 2014 policy implementation document issued by the central government through the State Council, whose version both differs and aligns with the Beijing Draft. Most significant of all, the State Council stressed that, as a policy, English is not to be separated from the main gaokao (known also as the unified gaokao) as called for by the Beijing Draft but is to remain as one of the core subjects to be examined. Furthermore, the original scores assigned to the examination are to be maintained "as is" for now. However, similar to the Beijing Draft, instead of occurring only once, the State Council has decreed that English is to be given twice a year, in June and January. Furthermore, individual provinces can continue to decide on the content of the two examinations. As of April 2016, nineteen provinces and municipalities, including Beijing, have released local reform plans to implement the Council's directives (Ministry of Education, 2016). The central government, through the State Council, is thus continuing the practice of giving provinces freedom to develop and/or select the English examinations to use.

Reasons for the Reform

The reasons behind the Beijing Draft and the State Council's policy implementation document can be determined from several factors. First, the October 2013 Draft was issued in anticipation of the Central Committee of the Communist Party of China (CCCPC) meeting in the following month of November. (CCCP meetings are important annual meetings at the highest levels of government where national policies and priorities are announced.) At that point in time, there was an expectation that, along with other national policies, a larger educational policy to reform the gāokǎo was to be articulated. In addition, the surrounding public discourse was dominated by rhetoric emphasizing education as the stepping stone toward achieving the "Chinese Dream," which was conceived as the attainment of personal well-being and national pride in all things Chinese. The Beijing Draft's call for undertaking reform by removing English from the central gāokǎo and relegating it to separate bi-annual examinations converged with this line of thinking. Had the Draft been adopted as policy, it would have contributed to altering of the public's perception of the central role that English has played in Chinese education over the years. Removal of English from the gāokǎo would have had the effect of affirming Mandarin, the national language, as the only language deserving the honor of being part of the gaokao. The Beijing Draft is thus a nod to the belief of some that instructional and learning time allocated to the English language has competed with instructional time for learning Mandarin. (The former has taken up the longest learning time span [nine to fifteen years, from third grade to graduate school] of all subjects.) A 2014 pilot survey of public opinion reaffirmed the belief by showing that the Beijing Draft had significant public support. Results from the survey indicated that out of the 220,000 respondents, 82.82 percent supported it in general with 82.79 percent, in particular, supporting reducing the number of "admissions points" allocated to English (Rui, 2014). It is evident that the survey respondents were calling for a change in the importance placed on the English language, particularly, as a pre-requisite for entrance into Chinese universities.

Be that as it may, on a larger scale, the fact the Chinese central government asserted its authority over the English language gaokao reform suggests its view that English language policies may be a means to address several of the continuing concerns regarding the gaokao itself. In particular, the bi-annual English examinations may be a means for the government to demonstrate sensitivity to the enormous pressure placed on students by the national testing program. In particular, in providing the option for students to take two English examinations and to use the higher of the two scores for admissions could be aimed at alleviating the long-lamented practice of having students take examinations on all subjects in a single, year-end examination period. College applicants are known to spend forty hours studying for the national examinations during the school week, ten hours after school, and for those who can afford it, additional hours with tutors during weekends.

The bi-annual English language examinations reform efforts could also be seen as national policy makers' reiteration of the need for communicative pedagogy to remain in the center of instruction (Yue, 2015). The pedagogy and the approaches in it were strongly promoted in the 2003 English Language Curriculum Standards have yet to be satisfactorily implemented. Currently, Chinese English language teachers (ELTs) spend a considerable part of the school year preparing students using teacher-centered knowledge transmission and "drill-and-kill" approaches. Public school English teachers typically focus on reductive knowledge and skill for short-term test preparation (Matoush & Fu, 2012) in English. Perhaps the thinking is that when year-end pressure of English examinations is removed (or at least dispersed), more classroom time could perhaps be spent on communicative activities, particularly task-based, problem solving and critical thinking, advocated in the national curriculum. The State Council's enforcement of the bi-annual examinations could be part of its effort to create room for teachers to incorporate these communicative activities more fully into instruction.

The State Council's September 2014 policy implementation document mentioned previously outlined the continuing practice of providing the option to provinces to individually determine the implementation of the English gaokao reform policy. In this regard, there is thus acknowledgment of deep-rooted problems in the national examination process itself, including a long-held concern that national examinations are inequitable because their contents are biased toward what is available, taught, and learned in urban populations such as Beijing and Shanghai. The inequity is especially acute for students in the more remote provinces where there is disparity in the resources available, students' access to information, and the availability of qualified teachers to prepare students for the national examinations. Partly as a means to rectify these inequities, bonus gāokǎo merit points are allocated to ethnic minority, underprivileged, and special needs students (Wong, 2012).

The implications of the English language gaokao reform effort will, of course, be seen in the near future as they are implemented. We are using the opportunity in this forum to explore both the challenges and opportunities that this policy reform may bring.

Possible Impact of the Reform

Obviously, one concern to some observers is whether the public will have a diminished view of the importance of English when its examination is broken up into two parts. This means that during the main gaokao period in June, the English examination will be incomplete in contrast to the examination of other subjects. If this perception prevails, it could also adversely affect motivation in studying the language and exacerbate the reported decline in China's English proficiency ranking. Indeed, in 2015, China's ranking had already dropped ten places from 37 to 47 in the English proficiency index covering seventy countries (Tan, 2015).

With the introduction of an additional English gaokao examination, it is entirely possible that many teachers will take even more time to focus on the English test preparation, minimizing opportunities to engage students in developing the highly sought after communicative skills that they have been mandated to incorporate into their curriculum and examinations. Furthermore, the reform at this point, does not mention any changes in the content of what is to be tested. If the status quo prevails, the tested content could still primarily cover receptive skills (listening and reading) rather than the productive skills of writing and speaking needed for communication. It is easy to see how such a situation could happen as communicative skills emerge from activities that are time-intensive as they are usually open-ended. As it is, when English is a part of the main gāokǎo at the end of the school year, teachers already begin early in the year to prepare for the examination and use up a large part of instructional time. As students will be doubly examined in English in the new reform policy, it is conceivable that teachers will spend more time preparing students to develop examination-passing skills that may or may not translate into communicative skills. Even "foreign" teachers or native speakers of English, who are often assigned to lead communicative classroom activities, may well find themselves needing to teach to the more frequently occurring examinations.

As mentioned earlier, the central government through the State Council maintains that the development and/or selection of English examinations to be used can be localized. In low-resourced and remote areas of the country, however, this may be a challenge as there is a shortage of proficient English teachers and qualified native speakers who can teach English. As it is, there is an overall need for an increase in the number of qualified Chinese English language teachers (ELTs). The faculty-to-student ratio in China, per population, is approximately 1 Chinese ELT to about 400 Chinese students (in the U.S., the norm is 1 teacher to 30 students). Teacher training is also uneven as Luo (2011) reported that 84 percent of college-level Chinese English teachers have had no overseas experiences, 83 percent had never attended an overseas conference, and about 40 percent had not attended any domestic conferences. The situation is exacerbated amongst public school teachers, particularly, in the rural areas where compared to their counterparts in resource-rich areas, they have limited exposure to the English language and fewer training opportunities in current teaching pedagogies (Hu, 2005; Gong & Holliday, 2015). Rural teachers report also lower wages, heavier workload as well as fewer chances for promotion in comparison to their urban counterparts, resulting in large teacher turnover in rural provinces (Liu & Onwuegbuzie, 2012). The situation creates a vacuum of qualified individuals who are available to develop examinations locally, in this regard, for the subject of English.

The localization of examination development also can lead to the non-uniformity of examination rigor and standards that could compromise fairness in evaluating student performance. Thus in reality, even though this localization option has always been available to provinces and municipalities, the common practice has been for them to use examinations that the central government identified and selected as exemplary. This is evidenced by the fact that at the point of the reform, more than half of the thirty-four Chinese provinces and four municipalities reported such a practice (Ministry of Education, 2016). Cognizant of this reality, the central government indicated that in developing and/or selecting examinations, it will defer to and draw from pilot examinations undertaken in Zhejiang Province and Shanghai municipality. However, it does remain a matter of significant concern that the two prominent and well-resourced areas are preferred locations to pilot the development of the new national English examinations. This is because English examinations resulting from pilot tests developed in these urban and well-resourced centers are not likely to represent the resources and skills available in the more remote and economically challenged sections of China.

It is reassuring, however, in its localization efforts, that the State Council's policy implementation directive continues the past practice of using government agencies from each locality for examination development. For example, in Shanghai, the Educational Examination Authority is one such agency. Otherwise, there is the fear that if entrepreneurial entities were allowed to get involved, profit-making interests could supersede the mission of making English examinations responsive to local contexts.

All in all, if the Chinese government through the State Council eventually decides to use this new reform to overhaul the content of English examinations in general, it could provide unprecedented opportunities to improve English language instruction in China. Productive and communicative skills of listening and speaking, when prioritized, can address the much-regretted and denigrating "deaf-and-dumb English" situation whereby it is said that even after 900 hours of instruction in public schools, Chinese students are not able to engage effectively in conversing extemporaneously in English (Wei & Su, 2012). The reform, if used to target such skills, could provide an incentive for teachers and students to devote more time in developing them. Perhaps also, in this way, it could relieve pressure on parents to send their children to private entrepreneurial schools such as Crazy English, Disney English, and Pop Kids English who laud their ability to teach English for communicative purposes. If the English reform, accompanied with teacher training, does lead to the enhancement of communicative proficiency, the new bi-annual English examinations could also contribute to a more seamless transition for Chinese students into domestic or overseas institutions where English is the medium of instruction.

As can be seen, the English gāokǎo reform has major implications for English language education and instruction. The reform is thus a call for professionals near and far in the field to pay close attention as to how it may affect their research and teaching practice.

References

Gong, F., & Holliday, A. (2015). Exploring the value of ELT as a secondary school subject in China: A multi-goal model for the English curriculum. In B. Spolsky & K. Sung (Eds.), *Secondary school English education in Asia* (pp. 201–218). New York, NY: Taylor & Francis.

Hé, D., & Zhāng, Q. (2010). Native speaker norms and China English: From the perspective of learners and teachers in China. *TESOL Quarterly, 44,* 769–789. doi: 10.5054/tq.2010.235995

Higgins, C. (2003). "Ownership" of English in the outer circle: An alternative to the NS-NNS dichotomy. *TESOL Quarterly, 37,* 615–644. doi: 10.2307/3588215

Hu, G. (2005). English language education in China: Policies, progress, and problems. *Language Policy, 4*(1), 5–24. doi: 10.1007/s10993-004-6561-7

The Implementation Opinions of the State Council on Deepening the Reform of Examination and Admission System. (2014). Retrieved from www.gov.cn/zhengce/content/2014-09/04/content_9065.html

Liú, Q. (2008). Development of NMET over the past thirty years. *Curriculum, Teaching Material and Method, 28*(4), 22–27.

Liu, S., & Onwuegbuzie, A. J. (2012). Chinese teachers' work stress and their turnover intention. *International Journal of Educational Research, 53,* 160–170. doi: 10.1016/j.ijer.2012.03.006

Luo, L. (2011, July 8). *On education in China: Its current situation, challenges, and future.* Paper presented at the TESOL Symposium in China, Beijing Normal University, Beijing, China.

Luo, W. (2015, Jan 1). False reports undermine institutions in the short term. *China Daily USA.* Retrieved from http://usa.chinadaily.com.cn/epaper/2015-01-01/content_19212338.htm

Matoush, M. M., & Fu, D. (2012). Examinations of English language as significant thresholds for college-bound Chinese and the washback of test-preparation. *Changing English: An International Journal of English Teaching, 19,* 111–121.

Meng, J. (2014, May 27). China focus: How do we say "bye bye" to English. *Xinhua News.* Retrieved from http://news.xinhuanet.com/english/china/2014-05/27/c_133365007.htm

Ministry of Education (MOE). (2003). *National curriculum standards album: English curriculum standards.* Retrieved from www.being.org.cn/ncs/eng/eng02.htm

Ministry of Education (MOE) (2016, April 26). 19 Provinces' new Gaokao reform plans, what are they? Retrieved from www.moe.gov.cn/jyb_xwfb/s5147/201604/t20160426_240183.html

Rui, Y. (2014). China's removal of English from *gaokao*. *International Higher Education, 75,* 12–13.

Tan, H. (2015, November 2). China is losing interest in learning English. *CNBC News.* Retrieved from www.cnbc.com/2015/11/02/china-boosts-chinese-usage-slips-in-global-english-proficiency-ranking.html

Wei, R., & Su, J. (2012). The statistics of English in China. *English Today, 28*(3), 10–14. doi: 10.1017/s0266078412000235

Wong, E. (2012, June 30). Test that can determine the course of life in China gets a closer examination. *The New York Times.* Retrieved from www.nytimes.com/2012/07/01/world/asia/burden-of-chinas-college-entrance-test-sets-off-wide-debate.html

Xiang, N. (2014, June 12). Gaokao English relegating to social exams: A survey result of 65.6% pros vs 15.0% cons. *China Youth Daily.* Retrieved from http://zqb.cyol.com/html/2014-06/12/nw.D110000zgqnb_20140612_2-07.htm

Yue, T. (2015, July 17). Gaokao revamp to stress better English. *The Telegraph.* Retrieved from www.telegraph.co.uk/sponsored/china-watch/society/11732022/chinese-gaokao-exams.html

Zhao, X. (2013, Dec 9). Gaokao reform removes English. *China Daily USA.* Retrieved from http://usa.chinadaily.com.cn/epaper/2013-12/09/content_17161917.htm

INDEX

achievement: shifu-tudi 54, 60–1; student 25, 72; teaching 84, 90, 92
The Analects of Confucius 53
Anyang Teachers College 11
Ausubel, David 100

Backbone Teacher 55–6, 87, 107
Bao Tian Ren Publishing House 128
Beijing Draft: description of 142–3; *see also* education reform
Beijing Lead Future Foundation 115
Beijing Municipal Education Commission (BMEC) 141
Beijing Normal University (BNU) 11, 13, 16, 29, 30, 108; case of Mozhi 33–4; curriculum 17; pre-service teacher training program 16–18
Beijing Tongxian Normal School 11
Beijing United Normal University 29
Blue Mountain Middle School (BMMS) 116; gains and opportunities 119–20; outcomes for rural teachers 119–21; profile of 117–18; teacher challenges 120–1; teacher trainer and institutional challenges 121–2; *see also* Sowers Action (SA)
Bush, George W. 6

case studies of student teaching: Chenxuan learning from others 34–6, 38; Mozhi showing expectations *vs* reality 32–4, 38; Taotao showing persistence and work ethic 36–8

Central China Normal University 108
central government, demanded professionalism 5–6
"Changing from Fish to Dragon" 1
Chen, Xin 2, 41–9, 125–39
China: English curriculum reform 112–14; English proficiency 145; governmental teacher policies 4–6; *see also* Ministry of Education (MOE)
China Scholarship Council (CSC): financial assistance for education 127–8; programs 128
Chinese Dream 125–7, 143
Chinese values 81–2
collaborative framework, Visiting Scholars Program (VSP) 137, 138
collectivism 81
Common Core Standards 7
competence 84
competitions *see* teacher competitions
Confucianism 10–11
Confucius 10–11, 21; shifu and tudi relationship 52–3
consecutive model, student teaching 29
constructionism 95
continuing professional stage 97
Cultural Revolution 5, 142

Daoism 10, 11, 13, 15
demanded professionalism 5–6
Deng Xiaoping 5, 126, 142

150 Index

diploma complimentary stage 97
distance education programs, Guo Pei Plan 104–5
Distance Education Project for Rural Schools (DEPRS) 104

East China Normal University 11, 13, 108
education reform: description of 142–3; possible impact of 145–7; reasons for 143–5
egalitarianism 81
English as a second/foreign language (ESL/EFL) 2–4
English gāokǎo reform 141–2; description of 142–3; possible impact of 145–7; reasons for 143–5
English language: instruction as subject 5; status in teacher training 20–2
English language standards: curriculum 144; examinations 146–7; goal description of nine levels 23–6; targets for teacher preparation 13–16
English language teachers (ELTs) 1–2, 3, 7; competitions among 81, 91, 95; jiaoyanzu's role in Chinese ELTs 68–9; obstacles of 111–14; professional development of 64, 98; requirements for, as visiting scholars 129–30; visiting scholar hopes 126; see also Sowers Action (SA); teacher competitions; Visiting Scholars Program (VSP)
Every Student Succeeds Act (ESSA) 7

Fan, Wenfang 2, 13, 41–9, 51–62, 64–78, 105; goal description of nine levels 23–6
Four Modernization and Open-Door Policy (1978) 5, 142
Four-Stage Model, Guo Pei Plan 100, 101
Fudan University 127
Fujian Normal School 16

government documents, shifu-tudi relationships 53
Guangzhou University 108
guanxi 82, 126
Guided Principles on Issues Concerning the First-time Teacher Certification (Ministry of Education) 42
Guo Pei Kindergarten Backbone Teacher Training 101–2
Guo Pei Plan 97, 114; approaches of 99–105; beginnings of National-Level Training Plan 98–9; considerations for next steps in 107–8; contextualized case-based teacher learning 100–1; distance education programs 104–5; Four-Stage Model 100; Guo Pei Kindergarten Backbone Teacher Training 101; knowledge-capability-practice-experience (KCPE) training model 100; national programs from 99; on-site classroom training model 102; Pedagogical Content Knowledge (PCK) concept 101–2; positions on, approaches 105–7; purpose of 106; teacher replacement 102–4; theoretical model application 99–102; Triangle Replacement Program 103; Western Backbone Teacher Training Program 102–3

Harbin Institute of Technology 127
He, Honghua 105
heart (*xin*) 84
Henan University 13
high-stakes competitions *see* teacher competitions
Hong Kong (HK) Sales Education Fund 104
How We Train Our Young Teachers (Lv) 53
Central China Normal University 11
hukou application: job security 45–6; permanent teachers 48–9
Hunan First Teacher College 16, 20

International English Language Testing System Examination (IELTS) 130
International Monetary Fund (IMF) 5
Interprofessional Collaboration Framework, D'Amour's model 137, 138
"Iron Rice Bowl": getting and staying in 42; term symbolizing jobs 41; *see also* permanent teacher qualifications

Jiangsu Normal University 108
Jiangxi Normal University 108
jiaoyanzu groups: reflection with peers 73–7; sociocultural perspective 68–9; teacher competitions 86–7; teacher development in 64–5; *see also* professional development
Jiaying University 103
Jin, Wei 2, 10–26, 28–39, 97–108
Journey to the West (Wu) 52

knowledge-capability-practice-experience (KCPE) model, Guo Pei Plan 100

Laozi 10, 21
learning, Ausubel's theory of 100
Luoyang Teachers College 11

master-novice relationship *see* shifu-tudi relationship
mentoring relationship: formal shifu-tudi 57; personal and informal 58; *see also* shifu-tudi relationship
mianzi 82
Mid-Western Backbone Teachers' Training Program 99, 100, 102–3
Ministry of Education (MOE): English curriculum reform 112–14; Guo Pei programs 105–6; international exchange and cooperation 126–7; permanent teaching jobs 42; Public English Test System (PETS) 130; public schools per student budget (2013) 112
Minsheng College 13
moral conduct 84

Nanjing University 127
Nanyang Normal School 11
Nanyang Teachers College 11
National College Entrance Examination (NCEE) 141
National-Level Training Plan, Guo Pei Plan 97–9
New Curriculum Reform (2011) 97
No Child Left Behind (NCLB) 6
non-governmental organizations (NGOs): role in communities 114–16; Sower Action (SA) teacher development project 115, 116–22; Summer Institute of Linguistics, Inc. (SIL) 115; Teach for China (TFC) 115; Zero Barrier Bilingual Education Project (ZBBEP) 115; *see also* Sowers Action (SA)
non-native English speaker teacher (NNEST) 1–2
Non-Profit Organizations (NPOs) 114; *see also* non-governmental organizations (NGOs)
normal schools, teacher training 11, 12
normal universities, teacher training 11, 12, 13
Northeast Normal University 11, 13

Obama, Barack 6
Olympic Games (2008) 5, 142
on-site classroom training model 102
overseas visiting programs: enablers for 127–9; sustainability of 135–7; *see also* Visiting Scholars Program (VSP)

paradoxical Chinese values 82
Pawan, Faridah 1–7, 2, 10–26, 64–78, 81–95, 125–39, 141–7
Pedagogical Content Knowledge (PCK) concept, Guo Pei Plan 101–2
pedagogy: English language 18–19, 22; language teaching 130, 144; student teaching 31, 33; teacher knowledge 42, 59, 68, 134
Pei, Miao 2, 10–26, 28–39, 97–108
Peking University 104, 108, 127
People's Daily (newspaper) 54
permanent teacher qualifications: critical thoughts of 47–9; getting and keeping jobs 42; hukou application process 48–9; importance of job 44; job offerings 44–7; problems of application process 48–9; salary 47; social position in Chinese culture 45; stability of job 45–6; teaching load 42–4
Personal Learning Networks (PLNs) 95
praxis, teacher expertise 3
Primary Backbone Headmaster Training 100–1
professional development 2–4; collaboration motivation 72; data coding and analysis 72–3; data collection 72; English language teachers (ELTs) 64, 78; Freeman and Johnson's tripartite sociocultural framework on teacher knowledge base 70, 74, 76; friendship with colleagues 73; *jiaoyanzu* peers 73–7; literature review 66–70; method 71–3; pressures on teachers 75–6; reflective teaching research 66–8; research question 71; research setting 64–5; sociocultural perspective on 68–9; students' struggles 74, 75; task-based teaching 74, 75; teacher demographic chart 71; teachers reflecting with peers 73–7; themes and focus areas 74
professionalism 2, 4–7; Chinese value 82; demanded 5; performance of teacher 48; reflective teaching 66
professionalization 4
Program for International Student Assessment (PISA) 6
Project of Exemplary Teachers Training (PETT) 114
Project of Rural Key Teacher Training (PRKTT) 114
Public English Test System (PETS) 130

Race to the Top (RTTP) 6
Reagan, Ronald 7

Index

reflective teaching, research 66–8
Renmin University of China 22
renqing 82
rural English teachers (RETs): Guo Pei Plan programs 114; improving English language skills of 123; obstacles for 112–14; outcomes with Sowers Action (SA) 119–21; per student budget for public schools 112; *see also* Sowers Action (SA)

school hierarchy, identification of shifu 54–6
Shandong Wendeng Normal School 11
Shanghai Jiao Tong 127
Shaanxi Normal University 13, 108
shifu: Backbone Teacher 55–6; identification of 54–6; Special Class Teacher 55–6; Subject Leading Figure 55–6; term 51
shifu-tudi relationship: background of 51–3; challenges and changes to system 60–2; in classroom practice 53–4; formal 57; identification of shifu 54–6; mentoring practices 54; official positions on 53; personal and informal 58; prospects of continuation 58–60; taxonomy of 56–62
shuti relationship 51; *see also* shifu-tudi relationship
sociocultural theory, teacher development 69
socio-professionals 3, 69
South China Normal University 108
Southwest University 13
Sowers Action (SA) 111, 115–16; Blue Mountain Middle School (BMMS) 116–22; establishment 115; gains and opportunities for BMMS 119–20; interviewees 116; metaphoric meaning of 115; outcomes for rural teachers 119–21; profile of BMMS 117–18; role in rural teacher development 114–16; teacher challenges at BMMS 120–1; teacher development project 116–22; teacher trainer and institutional challenges 121–2; teacher training projects 118
Special Class Teacher 55–6
State Council's policy implementation 143–7; *see also* education reform
student teaching 28, 39; case studies of experiences 32–8; Chenxuan case of learning from others 34–6, 38; Consecutive Model 29; demonstration classes 31–2; learning about themselves 38–9; models 28–30; Mozhi case showing expectations *vs* reality 32–4, 38; process of 30–2; Taotao case showing persistence and work ethic 36–8; teacher placement model 29
Subject Leading Figure 55–6
Summer Institute of Linguistics, Inc. (SIL) 115

Taiyuan Normal University 104
talking the talk 67
talking the walk 67
teacher: Action Research 94; Backbone Teacher 55–6; Chinese policies 4–6; formal shifu-tudi relationships 57; identification of shifu 54–6; principles of good teaching 84; professionalization *vs* professionalism 4; Special Class Teacher 55–6; Subject Leading Figure 55–6; U.S. government policies 6–7; *see also* permanent teacher qualifications; professional development; shifu-tudi relationship
Teacher Certification Regulations 5
teacher colleges, teacher training 11, 12, 16, 18
teacher competitions: competition as a paradox 81–3; criteria 85–6; critical look at 92–5; description 84–92; evaluation 88–90; organization and setting 86–8; outcomes of 90–2; paradoxical Chinese values 82; public lesson/competition organizers 87; supporting and sharing ideas 95; teacher excellence as a concept 83–4; teaching as a performance concept 93
teacher excellence, concept 83–4
teacher knowledge 3–4: Freeman and Johnson's tripartite framework on 70, 73, 74, 76; sociocultural perspective on 68–9
Teacher Law (1993) 5
"teacher replacement" model, student teaching 29
teacher policies, Chinese and U.S. 4–7
teacher replacement, Guo Pei programs 102–4, 106
Teachers' Law of the People's Republic of China 45
teacher training 2–4; Beijing Normal University (BNU) 16–18; Confucianism 10–11; current status of 20–2; curricula

coverage 16–18; Daoism 10, 11, 15; English language standards as targets in 13–16, 20–2; institutions 12; normal schools 11, 12; normal universities 11, 12, 13; pathways to pre-service 11, 13; pre-service experiences 18–20; teacher colleges 11, 12; theory and practice in 21–2; *see also* student teaching
Teach for America (TFA) 6
Teach for China (TFC) 115
TESOL Quarterly (journal) 95
Test of English as a Foreign Language (TOEFL) 130
Third International Mathematics and Science Study (TIMSS) 6
threat rigidity 4
Triangle Replacement Program 103
Tseng Hin Pei Charity Fund 105
Tsinghua University 104–5, 108, 127; recruitment information from primary school 139
tudi, term 51

UNESCO Children's Fund Program 108
United States, governmental teacher policies 6–7
University of Science and Technology of China 127

Visiting Scholars Program (VSP) 125, 127; challenges and obstacles 132–5; China Scholarship Council (CSC) programs 128; collaborative framework of 137, 138; description of 129–35; opportunities created in 131–2; overseas experiences 127–9; requirements for ELTs as visiting scholars 129–30; sustainability of overseas visiting programs 135–7

walking the talk 67
walking the walk 67
Wang, Ge 2, 41–9, 111–23
Wen Jiabao 13
World Trade Organization (WTO) 5, 142

Xi'an Jiaotong University 127
Xi Jinping 126
xin (heart) 84

Yang, Fang 105
Yin and Yang 82
Young (under 40) Backbone Teachers Program 127
Yuan, Niya 2, 141–7
Yunnan Normal University (YNU) 103
Yunnan Province, English teachers 112, 114

Zero Barrier Bilingual Education Project (ZBBEP) 115
Zhejiang University 127
zhongzi (seed teachers) 106
zone of proximal development (ZPD) 69